QUOTIDIAN

QUOTIDIAN

With Very Best Wishes from Gudrun Cable

December 1978

Compiled by **Gudrun Cable**

Portraits by **Joelle Smith**

Merry Christmas 1978

Dennie, Susan, Jennifer, Robert & Allison

TELESIS

Portland and Corvallis, Oregon

Printed in the United States of American by Artline Printing, Inc.
Composition by Royal Typesetting Service, Portland, Oregon

I am grateful to the following for permission to quote:

The Dial Press for *The Fire Next Time* by James Baldwin. Copyright 1963 by James Baldwin.
Doubleday, Inc. for *Up from Slavery*, by Booker T. Washington. Copyright renewed 1963 by Doubleday, Inc. and *The Caine Mutiny*, by Herman Wouk. Copyright 1951 by Herman Wouk.
Harcourt Jovanovich, Inc. for *Two Cheers for Democracy* by E.M. Forster. Copyright 1938, 1951 by E.M. Forster.
Little, Brown and Co. for *The Aristos*, by John Fowles. Copyright 1964 by John Fowles.
The Viking Press for "In Distrust of Merits" by Marianne Moore from *Collected Poems* of Marianne Moore. Copyright 1944, 1972 by Marianne Moore. *Henderson the Rain King*, by Saul Bellow. Copyright 1959 by Saul Bellow. "Search for Love" by D.H. Lawrence from *The Complete Poems* of D.H. Lawrence, edited by Vivian de Sola Pinto and F. Warren Roberts. Copyright 1964, 1971 by Angelo Ravagli and C.M. Weekley.
MacMillan Publishing Co., Inc. for "Advice to a Girl" by Sara Teasdale from *Collected Poems* of Sara Teasdale. Copyright 1933 by MacMillan Publishing Co., Inc. Copyright renewal 1961 by Guaranty Trust Co. of New York, Exr. Coward, McCann and Geoghgan, Inc. for *The Zoo Story* by Edward Albee. Copyright 1960 by Edward Albee.
McGraw-Hill Book Co. for *The Stress of Life* by Hans Selye. Copyright 1959 by Hans Seyle.
William Morrow and Co., Inc. for *Last Rights* by Marya Mannes.
Louis Nizer for *Between You and Me.* Copyright 1963 by Louis Nizer. W.W. Norton and Co., Inc. for *Letters to a Young Poet*, by Ranier Maria Rilke. Translated by M.D. Herter Norton. Copyright 1934 by W.W. Norton and Co., Inc. Copyright Renewed 1962 by M.D. Herter Norton. Revised Edition Copyright 1954 by W.W. Norton and Co., Inc. And *Don't Fall Off the Mountain*, by Shirley MacLaine. Copyright 1970 by Shirley MacLaine.
Pantheon Books, a Division of Random House, Inc. *Gift from the Sea*, by Anne Morrow Lindbergh. Copyright 1955, 1964 by Anne Morrow Lindbergh. *Baldur's Gate*, by Eleanor Clark. Copyright 1955 by Eleanor Clark. Random House, Inc. for *Getting Even*, by Woody Allen. Copyright 1966 by Woody Allen.
Harcourt Brace Jovanovich, Inc. for *Meridian* by Alice Walker.
Clifton Fadiman for *Any Number Can Play.*
John Cage for *M-Writings '69-'72.* Copyright 1973.
Vivian Murphy, Henry S. Dennis, Ralph Friedman, Jennifer Froistad, Gil Wilson, Eugene McCarthy, Eli Siegel, Thadeus Golas, William Stafford.

Philosophical Library, Inc. for *Kafka: The Torment of Man,* by R.M. Alberes and Pierre de Boisdeffre. Copyright 1968 by Philosophical Library, Inc.

Prentice-Hall, Inc. for *Earn Warren,* by Irving Stone. Copyright 1948, 1976 by Irving Stone.
G.P. Putnam's Sons for *Living it Up*, by George Burns. Copyright 1976 by George Burns.
Real People Press for *Gestalt Therapy Verbatim,* Copyright 1969.
Charles Scribner's Sons for *Death in the Afternoon,* by Ernest Hemingway. Copyright 1932 by Charles Scribner's Sons, renewed 1960 by Ernest Hemingway.
Simon and Schuster for *The Seventh Seal,* by Ingmar Bergman, from *Four Screen Plays* of Ingmar Bergman. Copyright 1960 by Ingmar Bergman. *Zorba the Greek,* by Nikos Kazantzakis. Copyright 1952 by Simon and Schuster.
Yale University Press for *The Courage to Be,* by Paul Tillich. Copyright 1952 by Yale University Press.

First Printing 1978

Telesis: 2922 N.E. 18th Avenue; Portland, Oregon 97212
        2130 N.W. 11th Street; Corvallis, Oregon 97330

To Doug,
and
Marya, Trevor and Austin

PRELUDE

Everything that happened that night needed to happen. Somehow. When you want to talk to someone badly enough, time, distance, and reality itself won't stand in your way. And I *did* so want to talk to Roger Mifflin, the proprietor in Christopher Morley's adventure, *The Haunted Bookshop*. I knew of no one with a greater passion for books and a greater inclination to quote them.

It was a warm Spring evening, but as I made my way down Gissing Street the chill of a long forgotten November fog engulfed me. Passing the shops with their Christmas decorations, I found what I suddenly realized had been my destination. A gas-lit street lamp in front of a converted brownstone enabled me to read the sign above the door.

>PARNASSUS AT HOME
>R. AND H. MIFFLIN
>BOOKLOVERS WELCOME!
>THIS SHOP IS HAUNTED

A quick current of familiarity rushed through me. Without a moment's hesitation I descended the stairs leading to the entrance. The bell rang gently as I opened the door, peered into the shop, and without a doubt, into the past. It was just as Christopher Morley had described it, warm and pervaded by a comfortable dusk, dimly-lit here and there by green-shaded lamps. Proceeding to the back of the shop, I passed rows of shelves towering out of sight: "History", "Poetry", "Philosophy", "Literature".... The space not devoted to shelves was cluttered with hand-written notes quoting the world's great writers. Remembering that my aim was to find the proprietor, I resisted the books and the quotes, and moved on.

It wasn't difficult finding him since a cloud of blue pipe smoke hung over one corner of the room. I pretended to be browsing as I followed the "Biography" section around the corner to catch a glimpse of him. His back to me, he sat reading at a desk piled high with papers and volumes of books. He was a small man, in his late 40's, and as bald as I had imagined him.

"You're looking for me, aren't you?" he asked without turning or even closing his book.

"How did you know?"

"It's a haunted bookshop, didn't you read the sign?" he laughed.

It suddenly dawned on me that I myself was haunting the shop. I was a ghost of the future and he seemed to know it. He swung his swivel chair around and stood to greet me. "I'm Roger Mifflin. Forgive me for teasing you, but I couldn't resist."

"I would have recognized you anywhere. Mr. Morley did such a good job of describing you. I'm really happy to meet you. Is Mrs. Mifflin here too?" I asked.

"Of course. I'll get her." He opened the door that led to their apartment in the back of the shop. "Helen, there's a young woman here who would like to meet you."

"Show her into the dining room and I'll bring out some cider and chocolate cake," came a cheerful voice.

Now anyone who knows anything about Helen Mifflin knows that her chocolate cake cannot be resisted. I joined them with virtually no coaxing. As I entered the room, I found myself staring at the antiquated furnishings and at Mrs. Mifflin's old fashioned flower-print dress and lace apron. She glanced at my blue jeans and Mozart tee shirt and smiled. "What did you say your name is my dear?"

"It's Gudrun Cable, but my family and friends have always called me Goody."

"And I'm Helen Mifflin. Now come along to the fire and get warm. I'm afraid you've forgotten to dress for Brooklyn."

"Or for November," I added. I hadn't really noticed that I'd been shivering, but I was. I wondered if it was the cold.

In a few minutes we were comfortably seated at the dining room table partaking of the refreshments and enjoying the warmth of the fire.

In no time the conversation turned to books, and I explained my own plans to publish *this* book. They were curious as to why it was designed to promote discussion at the dinner table.

"Why that's probably the most important part of the day, for us!" insisted Roger. "We share what we've done, what we believe, how we feel. And is there a better way of getting to know your friends? You can't really get to know someone unless you've spent several invigorating hours with him at the dinner table!"

"Oh, Mr. Mifflin. In my day, few people will take the time. They often don't eat together let alone talk to one another. They're too busy watching television."

"Watching what?" asked Helen.

"Never mind," I sighed, "It's best you never know."

"Well, you certainly have come to the right person for help with quotations. Roger reads incessantly and he loves to share what he reads."

"Why I could give you hundreds of quotes from Carlisle alone!" he boasted.

"I don't need a hundred. In fact, I'm only using one quote for each day of the year and that quote has to be from someone born on that day."

"I see. Then you've probably chosen Benjamin Franklin for January 6th?" asked Roger.

"Actually, I'm using him on January 17th, the Gregorian Calendar date. Both are equally valid and I want to quote Alan Watts on January 6th."

"Who on earth is Alan Watts?" asked Helen.

"Oh, I forgot. If this is 1918 then he's approximately three years old and is hardly quotable yet!"

"365 people born on 365 days won't be easy to find," said Roger.

"No, it won't be easy. And I'm using 367 days as the book will include February 29th and a special day of my own. But don't ask me where I'm putting it because I won't tell you!"

By this time Roger was totally intrigued and was obviously eager to help. "By the Bones of Charles Lamb, what fun you must be having! There must be something I can do for you. Just name it!"

"Mostly I would like advice on books to read and authors who shouldn't be left out. Surely you're familiar with names I've probably never heard of. I want a large variety of topics and many different schools of thought. There should be diverse viewpoints on love and war and knowledge and religion and history. I want it to be impossible for any one person to agree with every quote in the book."

"A clever approach!" declared Roger. "I oftentimes find a great deal more pleasure in confronting opinions I disagree with or that anger me.''

"You should see him, Goody. His ears turn pink, his blue eyes sparkle, his words seem to chase the ideas around his head!''

"I have so many books that you absolutely must read,'' said Roger, in an attempt to change the subject. He jumped up from his chair and quickly scanned his personal bookshelves that lined the dining room walls. He shouted out titles and authors as he piled the books before me. *The Letters of Flaubert, The Poetry of Austin Dobson, Samuel Pepys' Diary, The Essays of Sainte-Beuve.''*

As I thumbed through the books I found small pieces of paper marking pages to read or passages he wished to remember. That dear little gentleman was pouring gold before me.

Helen laughed, "I'm having a hard time deciding which of the two of you is enjoying this more!''

I thought for an instant of my own children on Christmas morning, and how they're torn between ripping open new packages, playing with the ones they've opened, or showing them off to one another. We were certainly not at all unlike them, yet we were dealing with the wisdom of the ages and they with little plastic boats and planes. "No gift can be too large or too small if it brings joy,'' I thought out loud.

"And there is no gift,'' Roger continued my thought, "that can bring more joy than sharing knowledge. Strangely enough, I think the person who actually does the sharing receives the greatest gift.''

"What a quotable thing to say! Tell me, Mr. Mifflin, when is your birthday?''

Roger smiled at Helen and then shrugged his shoulders. "Mr. Morley never gave me one.''

"I'm terribly sorry. I should have known better.''

Our conversation wandered throughout the course of history, literature, and the civilization of mankind in general. At one point Helen asked to see my little yellow notebook where I keep lists of birthdays and favorite quotations. The two of them read aloud several of the quotes and inquired about people unknown to their time. Mr. Mifflin was constantly on his feet hunting for books or passages.

"You really must borrow my translation of Joubert. I think it's much better than the one you've been reading,'' he said.

I wondered if I *were* to borrow the book how I'd ever return it to him. I couldn't exactly put it in the mail. And how was I to know if I'd ever be able to find Gissing Street again. I simply told him how wonderful I thought it was that he was so generous with his books.

"To me books are living spirits and not material objects," he said. "They, like the characters in them, survive only when they are made part of the reader's life."

He looked up, and as our eyes met he sensed my gratitude and love. In that brief exchange, he acknowledged that he, too, understood the significance of our meeting. My first impulse was to run and tell Martin Buber what I had just experienced. But that's an impulse I often have.

"I'm afraid I must be going," I finally said.

"It's up to you. You know the choice is yours. It always belongs to the reader."

I made my way quickly to the front of the shop, feeling the living quarters, the dining room, dissolve. As I went outside and closed the door behind me, the doorknob gently slipped out of my hand. The door didn't latch shut, the bell didn't ring, there were no voices bidding me a pleasant good evening. As I walked up the small flight of stairs that led to Gissing Street each step seemed to disintegrate beneath my feet. I noted that the gas-lit street lamp had become an ordinary electric bulb. I reached up, turned it off, closed the book and for a while sat alone in the dark.

No one ever regarded the first of January with indifference.

Charles Lamb

January 1

E.M. Forster
(b. 1879 - d. June 7, 1970)
English Novelist

What is good in people — and consequently in the world — is their insistence on creation, their belief in friendship and loyalty for their own sakes; and though Violence remains and is, indeed, the major partner in this muddled establishment, I believe that creativeness remains too, and will always assume direction when violence sleeps.

What I Believe

January 2

William Lyon Phelps
(b. 1865 - d. August 21, 1943)
American Educator

As we grow older, we are less and less likely to call others insane.

Human Nature

January 3

Marcus Tullius Cicero
(b. 106B.C. - d. December 7,43B.C.)
Roman Philosopher

Life's race-course is fixed; Nature has only a single path and that path is run but once, and to each stage of existence has been allotted its own appropriate quality; so that the weakness of childhood, the impetuosity of youth, the seriousness of middle life, the maturity of old age — each bears some of Nature's fruit, which must be garnered in its own season.

de Senectute

January 4

A.E. Coppard
(b. 1878 - d. January 13, 1957)
English Poet and Short Story Writer

Morality...what is it but agreement with your own soul?

"Dusky Ruth"

January 5

Humbert Wolfe
(b. 1885 - d. January 5, 1940)
English Poet

All poets fail. That is why there is always room for another.

Dialogues and Monologues

January 6

Alan Watts
(b. 1915 - d. November 16,1973)
American Philosopher

For unless one is able to live fully in the present, the future is a hoax. There is no point whatever in making plans for a future which you will never be able to enjoy. When your plans mature, you will still be living for some other future beyond. You will never, never be able to sit back with full contentment and say, "Now, I've arrived!" Your entire education has deprived you of this capacity because it was preparing you for the future, instead of showing you how to be alive now.

The Book

January 7

Charles Peguy
(b. 1873 - d. September 5,1914)
French Writer

Any father whose son strikes him is guilty: of having conceived a son capable of striking him.

Basic Verities

January 8

Pamela Frankau
(b. 1908 - d. June 8,1967)
English Novelist

The important thing for me, always, has been to go on,
to keep at it; not to let the slack periods, the interim
dryness nor even the well-earned holiday rust the tools.
They rust all too easily.

Pen to Paper - A Novelist's Notebook

January 9

Simone de Beauvoir
(b. 1908 -   )
French Writer

Live with no time out.

All Said and Done

January 10

Robinson Jeffers
(b. 1887 - d. January 20, 1962)
American Poet

...the calm to look for is the calm at the whirlwind's heart.

Be Angry at the Sun

January 11

William James
(b. 1842 - d. August 26, 1910)
American Psychiatrist

Everyone feels that his total *power* rises when he passes to a higher "qualitative" level of life. Writing is higher than walking, thinking is higher than writing, deciding higher than thinking, deciding "no" higher than deciding "yes"....

Memories and Studies

William James

January 12

Jack London
(b. 1876 - d. November 22, 1916)
American Novelist

Everything is good...as long as it is unpossessed. Satiety and possession are Death's horses; they run in span.

When God Laughs

January 13

G.I. Gurdjieff
(b. 1872 - d. October 29, 1949)
Russian Mystic

A true sign of a good man is if he loves his father and mother.

Views from the Real World

January 14

Albert Schweitzer
(b. 1875 - d. September 4, 1965)
German Scholar and Humanitarian

...when people have light in themselves, it will shine out from them. Then we get to know each other as we walk together in the darkness, without needing to pass our hands over each other's faces, or to intrude into each other's hearts.

Memoirs of Childhood and Youth

January 15

Martin Luther King
(b. 1929 - d. April 4, 1968)
American Clergyman and Civil Rights Leader

Freedom is never voluntarily given by the oppressor;
it must be demanded by the oppressed.

I Have a Dream

January 16

Nigel Dennis
(b. 1912 -   )
English Novelist

Like everyone who is not at home in contemporary
society, I spin out the most ingenious theories to prove
either that everyone was once like me or that everyone
will be, in years to come.

Card of Identity

January 17

Benjamin Franklin
(b. 1706 - d. April 17, 1790)
American Publisher

...if you teach a poor young man to shave himself and keep his razor in order, you may contribute more to the happiness of his life than in giving him a thousand guineas.

Autobiography

January 18

Austin Dobson
(b. 1840 - d. September 2, 1921)
English Poet

Love comes unseen; we only see it go.

"The Story of Rosina"

January 19

Paul Cezanne
(b. 1839 - d. October 22, 1906)
French Artist

You have no idea how life-giving it is to find around one a youth that agrees not to bury one on the spot.

Quoted by Joachim Gasquet

January 20

George Burns
(b. 1895 -)
American Entertainer

I think the trouble with a lot of people is that they work too hard at staying married. They make a business out of it. When you work too hard at a business you get tired; and when you get tired you get grouchy; and when you get grouchy you start fighting; and when you start fighting you're out of business.

Living it Up

January 21

Stonewall Jackson
(b. 1824 - d. May 5, 1863)
American General

Resolve to perform what you ought; perform without fail what you resolve.

Quoted by Frank E. Vandiver

January 22

Lord Byron
(b. 1788 - d. April 19, 1824)
English Poet

He who ascends to mountain tops shall find
The loftiest peaks most wrapt in clouds and snow;
He who surpasses or subdues mankind,
Must look down on the hate of those below.

"Childe Harold"

January 23

Hugh Prather
(b. 1938 -   )
American Writer

No one is wrong. At most someone is uninformed.
If I think a man is wrong, either I am unaware of
something, or he is. So unless I want to play a superior-
ity game I had best find out what he is looking at.

Notes to Myself

January 24

Edith Wharton
(b. 1862 - d. August 12,1937)
American Novelist

The law represents material rights — it can't go beyond.
If we don't recognize an inner law...the obligation that
love creates...being loved as well as loving...there is
nothing to prevent our spreading ruin unhindered...
is there?

The Reckoning

January 25

Somerset Maugham
(b. 1874 - d. December 16, 1965)
English Writer

There is only one freedom that is really important and that is economic freedom, for in the long run the man who pays the piper calls the tune.

The Constant Wife

January 26

Hans Selye
(b. 1907 -   )
Canadian Physician

The most acquisitive person is so busy reinvesting that he never learns how to cash in. "Realistic people" who pursue "practical aims" are rarely as realistic and practical, in the long run of life, as the dreamers who pursue only their dreams.

The Stress of Life

January 27

Lewis Carroll
(b. 1832 - d. January 14,1898)
English Writer

"If you knew Time as well as I do," said the Hatter, "you wouldn't talk about wasting *it*. It's *him*."

"I don't know what you mean," said Alice.

"Of course you don't!" the Hatter said, tossing his head contemptuously. "I dare say you never even spoke of Time!"

"Perhaps not," Alice cautiously replied, "but I know I have to beat time when I learn music."

"Ah! That accounts for it," said the Hatter, "He won't stand beating."

Alice in Wonderland

January 28

Susan Sontag
(b. 1933 -   )
American Writer

...it is a far simpler matter to plot and commit a crime than it is to live with it afterwards.

Against Interpretation

Lewis Carroll

January 29

Thomas Paine
(b. 1737 - d. June 8, 1809)
American Pamphleteer

That which may be thought right and found convenient in one age, may be thought wrong and found inconvenient in another. In such cases, who is to decide, the living, or the dead?

Rights of Man

January 30

Walter Savage Landor
(b. 1775 - d. September 17, 1864)
English Writer

Love is a secondary passion to those who love most, a primary passion for those who love least.

Quoted by Glenway Wescott

January 31

Thomas Merton
(b. 1915 - d. December 10, 1968)
American Cleric

Those who love their own noise are impatient of everything else. They constantly defile the silence of the forests and the mountains and the sea. They bore through silent nature in every direction with their machines, for fear that the calm world might accuse them of their own emptiness.

No Man is an Island

Now it was February, the month of winds, freezing hopes and lamentations, and the rain gabbled against the window-panes.

Edward Dahlberg

February 1

Langston Hughes
(b. 1902-d. May 22, 1967)
American Poet

Hold fast to dreams
For if dreams die
Life is a broken-winged bird
That cannot fly.

"Dreams"

Langston Hughes

February 2

Havelock Ellis
(b. 1858 - d. August 24, 1943)
English Writer

Man is a gregarious animal, the creature of his small flock, inimical, at best indifferent, to all other flocks. If Nature needs a truly sympathetic international animal, Nature must wipe out Man and produce another species.

The Art of Life

February 3

Simone Weil
(b. 1909 - d. August 24, 1943)
French Writer

So long as one is prevented by pride from being willing to receive, one has no right to give.

First and Last Notebooks

February 4

Dietrich Bonhoeffer
(b. 1906 - d. April 9, 1945)
German Pastor

We must not wallow in our memories or surrender to them, just as we don't gaze all the time at a valuable present, but get it out from time to time, and for the rest hide it away as a treasure we know is there all the time. Treated in this way, the past can give us lasting joy and inspiration.

Letters and Papers from Prison

February 5

Adlai Stevenson
(b. 1900 - d. July 14, 1965)
American Statesman

We shall not love our corner of the planet less for loving the planet too, and resisting with all our skill and passion the dangers that would reduce it to smoldering ashes.

Address of December 18, 1963

February 6

Louis Nizer
(b. 1902 -   )
American Lawyer

...we are living in an age chiefly fit for youth, for it requires limitless imagination and courage. Every castle on earth was once a castle in the air.

Between You and Me

February 7

Charles Dickens
(b. 1812 - d. June 9, 1870)
English Novelist

It would be well, there can be no doubt, for the American people as a whole, if they loved the real less and the ideal somewhat more. It would be well, if there were greater encouragement to lightness of heart and gaiety, and a wider cultivation of what is beautiful, without being eminently and directly useful.

American Notes

February 8

Martin Buber
(b. 1878 - d. June 13, 1965)
Jewish Religious Philosopher

As the hand held before the eye hides the tallest mountain, so this small earthly life hides from our gaze the vast radiance and secrets of which the world is full, and whoever can take life from before his eyes, as one takes away one's hand, will see the great radiance within the world.

To Hallow This Life

February 9

Alice Walker
(b. 1944 -   )
American Novelist

Grown-up white men don't want to pretend to be anything else. Not even for a minute.

Meridian

Martin Buber

February 10

Bertolt Brecht
(b. 1898 - d. August 14, 1956)
German Playwright

As regards obstacles, the shortest distance between two points can be a curve.

Galileo

February 11

Lydia Maria Child
(b. 1802 - d. October 20, 1880)
American Reformer

Nature made us *individuals,* as she did the flowers and the pebbles; but we are afraid to be peculiar, and so our society resembles a bag of marbles, or a string of mould candles.   Why should we all dress after the same fashion?   The frost never paints my windows twice alike.

Letter of March 17, 1843

February 12

Abraham Lincoln
(b. 1809 - d. April 15, 1865)
United States President

As I would not be a slave, so I would not be a master.
This expresses my idea of democracy. Whatever differs
from this, to the extent of the difference, is no democracy.

Speech of August 1, 1858

February 13

John La Farge
(b. 1880 - d. November 24, 1963)
American Cleric

For those who believe in God no explanation is needed;
for those who do not believe in God no explanation is
possible.

The Manner is Ordinary

February 14

George Jean Nathan
(b. 1882 - d. April 8, 1958)
American Writer

After a long and uninterrupted period of serious regard
of anything, the wind always changes and there is
born a sudden and recalcitrant laughter. Human nature
is such that it cannot stand monotony; it demands relief.

Land of the Pilgrim's Pride

February 15

Alfred North Whitehead
(b. 1861 - d. December 30, 1947)
English Philosopher

It requires a very unusual mind to undertake the
analysis of the obvious.

Science and the Modern World

February 16

Henry Brooks Adams
(b. 1838 - d. March 27, 1918)
American Historian

...a boy's will is his life, and he dies when it is broken, as the colt dies in harness, taking a new nature in becoming tame.

The Education of Henry Adams

February 17

Dorothy Canfield Fisher
(b. 1879 - d. November 9, 1958)
American Writer

...there are two ways to meet life; you may refuse to care until indifference becomes a habit, a defensive armor, and you are safe — but bored. Or you can care greatly, and live greatly — till life breaks you on its wheel.

The Deepening Stream

February 18

John Ruskin
(b. 1819 - d. January 20, 1900)
English Art Critic

...all truth that makes us smile is partial.

Precious Thoughts

February 19

Carson McCullers
(b. 1917 - d. September 30, 1967)
American Novelist

...when hurt has been caused by a loved one, only the loved one can comfort.

Clock Without Hands

February 20

Georges Bernanos
(b. 1888 - d. July 5, 1948)
French Novelist

This world does not protect anyone; it offers security to no one; it no longer defends a single person. On the contrary, it is the world which needs to be defended, the world which we must save.

The Last Essays of Georges Bernanos

February 21

Anais Nin
(b. 1903 - d. January 14, 1977)
American Writer

...no one has ever loved an adventurous woman as they have loved adventurous men.

Diary, Volume I

February 22

Arthur Schopenauer
(b. 1788 - d. September 21, 1860)
German Philosopher

Belief is like love: it cannot be compelled; and as any attempt to compel love produces hate, so it is the attempt to compel belief which first produces real unbelief.

Essays and Aphorisms

February 23

Walter Bagehot
(b. 1826 - d. March 24, 1877)
English Political Analyst

Property is, indeed, a very imperfect test of intelligence; but it is some test. If it has been inherited, it guarantees education; if acquired it guarantees ability.

Introduction to *Historical Essays*

February 24

George Moore
(b. 1852 - d. January 21, 1933)
Irish Novelist

What I spent I had
What I saved I lost,
What I gave I have.

Quoted by Samuel Smiles

February 25

Mary Chase
(b. 1907 -   )
American Playwright

"Dr. Chumley, my mother used to say to me...'in this world, Elwood, you must be oh, so smart or oh, so pleasant.' For years I was smart. I recommend pleasant."

Harvey

February 26

Victor Hugo
(b. 1802 - d. May 22, 1885)
French Writer

Nature divides living beings into the coming and the going. The going are turned towards the shadow, the coming towards the light.

Les Miserables

February 27

John Steinbeck
(b. 1902 - d. December 20, 1968)
American Novelist

The things we admire in men, kindness and generosity, openness, honesty, understanding and feeling are the concomitants of failure in our system. And those traits we detest, sharpness, greed, acquisitiveness, meanness, egotism and self-interest are the traits of success. And while men admire the quality of the first they love the produce of the second.

Cannery Row

February 28

Vaslav Nijinsky
(b. 1890 - d. April 8, 1950)
Russian Dancer

I know that thought without logic has no value, but logic cannot exist without feeling.

Diary

February 29

George Seferis
(b. 1900 - d. September 20, 1971)
Greek Poet, Essayist, Diplomat

In my youth I had a tendency to jot down moments of distress. Perhaps it's progress: I now feel sorry when I note that the expansion of joy didn't impel me as easily toward paper.

A Poet's Journal

William Dean Howells

March is principally immense for wind,
but where it all comes from, and where
it all goes to, are prize conundrums
which I can't untangle.

Josh Billings

March 1

William Dean Howells
(b. 1837 - d. May 10, 1920)
American Novelist

A friend knows how to allow for mere quantity in
your talk, and only replies to the quality, separates
your earnest from your whimsicality, and accounts for
some whimsicality in your earnest.

A Modern Instance

March 2

John Jay Chapman
(b. 1862 - d. November 4, 1933)
American Essayist and Poet

An ignorant man makes a fortune and demands the higher education for his children. But it is too late; he should have given it to them when he was in his shirt sleeves. All that they are able to receive now is something very different from education.

"Learning"

March 3

Stephen A. Mitchell
(b. 1903 - d. April 23, 1974)
American Lawyer

The trouble with politics is that it is too much of a spectator's sport.

Elm Street Politics

March 4

Gil Wilson
(b. 1907 -   )
American Artist and Writer

I don't know what are the drives in an artist. Something is at work in him — like a ferment. He has accumulated something which is the common knowledge and feelings of many people. Through him, something called human experience finds an outlet. And in this expression there is maintained an inviolable and infinitely enduring identity among all human beings everywhere. This is the simple wonder of art.

Letter of March 6,1978

March 5

Frank Norris
(b. 1870 - d. October 25,1902)
American Novelist

"Death and grief are little things," he said. "They are transient. Life must be before death, and joy before grief. Else there are no such things as death or grief. These are only negatives."

The Octapus

March 6

Elizabeth Barrett Browning
(b. 1806 - d. June 29, 1861)
English Poet

If thou must love me, let it be for naught
    Except for love's sake only.

Sonnets of the Portuguese

March 7

Luther Burbank
(b. 1849 - d. April 11, 1926)
American Naturalist

The thing that binds all life together...is the cell from which all life springs and of which all life is made up. You cannot study plants without learning something about men, nor study men without getting ideas about animals and fish and plants.

The Harvest of the Years

March 8

Oliver Wendell Holmes
(b. 1841 - d. March 6, 1935)
American Jurist

A word is not a crystal, transparent and unchanged; it is the skin of a living thought and may vary greatly in color and content according to the circumstances and the time in which it is used.

Quoted by Catherine Drinker Bowen

March 9

Haniel Long
(b. 1888 - d. October 17, 1956)
American Educator

If one lives where all suffer and starve, one acts on one's own impulse to help. But where plenty abounds, we surrender our generosity, believing that our country replaces us each and several. This is not so, and indeed a delusion. On the contrary the power of maintaining life in others, lives within each of us, and from each of us does it recede when unused. It is a concentrated power.

The Power Within Us

March 10

Michel Eyquem de Montaigne
(b. 1533 - d. September 12, 1592)
French Writer

In my opinion the most profitable and most natural exercise of our mind is *conversation*. To me it is a more agreeable occupation than any other in life; and for that reason, if I were at this moment obliged to choose, I would sooner consent, I think, to lose my sight than my hearing or speech.

"Art of Conversation"

March 11

Ezra Jack Keats
(b. 1916 -   )
American Author and Illustrator

I trained myself by experimenting. I first realized that my drawings meant something when one day I covered our enamel-topped kitchen table with a host of sketches. My mother came in, and I expected her to say, "What have you been doing?" or "Get the sponge and wash off that table!" Instead she said, "Did *you* do that? Isn't it wonderful!" Rather than washing it off, she covered it with a tablecloth and showed it off period-ically to the neighbors and friends who visited her.

Interview in *Books Are by People*

March 12

Edward Albee
(b. 1928 -   )
American Playwright

Sometimes a person has to go a very long distance out of his way to come back a short distance correctly.

The Zoo Story

March 13

Paul Morand
(b. 1888 - d. July 23, 1976)
French Writer

Speed...kills colour; the gyroscope, when turning at full speed, shows up gray.

Papiers d'Identite

March 14

Albert Einstein
(b. 1879 - d. April 18,1955)
German/American Scientist

Many times a day I realize how much my own outer and inner life is built upon the labors of my fellow-men, both living and dead, and how earnestly I must exert myself in order to give in return as much as I have received. My peace of mind is often troubled by the depressing sense that I have borrowed too heavily from the work of other men.

Living Philosophies

March 15

William Lamb Melbourne
(b. 1779 - d. November 24,1848)
English Statesman and Prime Minister

Labor is so necessary to the health and vigor of the body, and consequently of the mind, that those, who by their wealth are exempted from it as a means of subsistence, are yet compelled to seek it as a diversion.

Quoted by David Cecil

Albert Einstein

March 16

Michelangelo
(b. 1475 - d. February 12, 1564)
Italian Artist

A beautiful thing never gives so much pain as does failing to hear and see it.

Michelangelo: A Self Portrait

March 17

Corra May Harris
(b. 1869 - d. February 9, 1935)
American Writer

...we only remember how beautiful we felt when we were young, whether we were or not.

My Book and Heart

March 18

John Updike
(b. 1932 -   )
American Writer

There is no goodness, without belief. There is nothing but busy-ness. And if you have not believed, at the end of your life you shall know you have buried your talent in the ground of this world and have nothing saved, to take into the next.

The Poorhouse Fair

March 19

Earl Warren
(b. 1891 - d. July 9, 1974)
American Journalist

If it is a mistake of the head and not the heart don't worry about it, that's the way we learn.

Quoted by Irving Stone

March 20

Ovid
(b. 43 B.C. - d. 18 A.D.)
Roman Poet

Seeking is all very well, but holding requires greater talent: Seeking involves some luck; now the demand is for skill.

Book II, *Art of Love*

March 21

Jean Paul Richter
(b. 1763 - d. November 14, 1825)
German Humorist and Poet

Only weak, caterpillar- and hedgehog-like souls curl and crumple up into themselves at every touch; under the free brain beats gladly a free heart.

Titan

March 22

Robert Millikan
(b. 1868 - d. December 19, 1953)
American Physicist

Perhaps the Mad Hatter had a reason for calling time Him.

Time, Matter and Value

March 23

Erich Fromm
(b. 1900 -   )
American Psychiatrist

To love one person productively means to be related to his human core, to him as representing mankind. Love for one individual, in so far as it is divorced from love for man, can refer only to the superficial and to the accidental; of necessity it remains shallow.

Man for Himself

March 24

William Morris
(b. 1834 - d. October 3, 1896)
English Poet, Artist, Manufacturer

Have nothing in your house that you do not know to be useful or believe to be beautiful.

The Beauty of Life

March 25

Gloria Steinem
(b. 1936 -   )
American Journalist and Feminist Leader

...male-female role-playing itself is probably the greatest long-term threat to peace. Anthropologists have found that the few societies without war are those in which sex roles are clear but not polarized. Women needn't be submissive semi-adults to be women, and men don't have to go to war or dominate their surroundings to be men.

"Why We Need a Woman President in 1976"

March 26

Robert Frost
(b. 1874 - d. January 29, 1963)
American Poet

Most of the change we think we see in life
Is due to truths being in and out of favor.

"The Black Cottage"

March 27

Budd Schulberg
(b. 1914 -   )
American Author

...my study of history has convinced me that in every strong and healthy society from the Egyptians to our own, the mass had to be guided with a strong hand by a responsible elite. Of course in our good country we cannot admit that....But let's not forget that in T.V. we have the greatest instrument for mass persuasion in the history of the world.

A Face in the Crowd

March 28

Maxim Gorky
(b. 1868 - d. June 18, 1936)
Russian Writer

Go on telling a man that he is a good man, and he will *be* good.

Fragments from My Diary

March 29

Eugene McCarthy
(b. 1916 -   )
American Senator

Beware of the politician with no further ambition.

Personal Conversation May 1976

March 30

Vincent Van Gogh
(b. 1853 - d. July 29, 1890)
Dutch Artist

The truth is that whenever two people love the same thing and work at it together, their union makes strength; combined, they can do more than if their separate energies were each striving in a different direction. By working together one becomes stronger and the whole is formed....

Letter of January 1883

March 31

John Fowles
(b. 1926 -   )
British Novelist

Show the young sailor how to sail; but don't so falsify the compass and the chart that he can sail only in one direction.

The Aristos

April 1

Agnes Repplier
(b. 1855 - d. December 15, 1950)
American Writer

Every nation is convinced that she is dedicated to peace; but that the actions of other nations are open to suspicion. Every system of government is warranted by its upholders to insure harmonious relations, while every other system must lead inevitably to war.

Times and Tendencies

April 2

Gladys Taber
(b. 1899 -   )
American Writer

In grief, one can endure the day, just the day. But when one also tries to bear the grief ahead, one cannot compass it. As for happiness, it can only be the ability to experience the moment. It is not next year that life will be so flawless and if we keep trying to wait for next year's happiness, the river of time will wind past and we shall not have lived at all.

Stillmeadow Day Book

April 3

Washington Irving
(b. 1783 - d. November 28, 1859)
American Writer

There is a certain relief in change, even though it be from bad to worse; as I have found in travelling in a stage-coach, that it is often a comfort to shift one's position and be bruised in a new place.

Tales of a Traveller

April 4

Remy de Gourmont
(b. 1858 - d. September 27, 1915)
French Writer

In order to understand life it is not only necessary not to be indifferent to men, but not to be indifferent to flocks, to trees. One should be indifferent to nothing.

Philosophic Nights in Paris

April 5

Booker T. Washington
(b. 1856 - d. November 14, 1915)
American Educator

I have learned that success is to be measured not so much by the position that one has reached in life as by the obstacles which he has overcome while trying to succeed.

Up From Slavery

April 6

Lincoln Steffens
(b. 1866 - d. August 9, 1936)
American Journalist

Strange that the politer the society, the greater the lies it requires.

Lincoln Steffens Speaking

April 7

Joshua Loth Liebman
(b. 1907 - d. June 9, 1948)
Jewish Religious Leader

Excessive competitiveness, anxiety, hostility, suspiciousness, all originate in the nursery years. That is why, if we want a world of peace and not violence, love and not hate, cooperation and not murder, justice and not selfishness, we have to learn how to make childhood more happy. No nobler task could be pursued by our generation.

Hope for Man

April 8

Baynard Kendrick
(b. 1894 -   )
American Novelist

...the love of a woman who runs away from the things she loves best because she knows that to stay is wrong is the strongest love in the world that a man can find.

The Flames of Time

April 9

Charles Baudelaire
(b. 1831 - d. August 31, 1867)
French Poet

...it is more difficult to love God than to believe in Him.

Flowers of Evil

April 10

William Hazlitt
(b. 1778 - d. September 18, 1830)
English Writer

Many a man has been hindered from pushing his fortune in the world by an early cultivation of his moral sense and has repented of it at leisure during the rest of his life.

Table Talk

April 11

Leo Rosten
(b. 1908 -   )
American Writer

I learned that it is the weak who are cruel, and that gentleness is to be expected only from the strong.

Captain Newman, M.D.

April 12

Alan Ayckbourn
(b. 1939 -   )
British Playwright

Some women...enjoy tremendously being told they look a mess — and they actually thrill to the threat of physical violence. I've never met one that does, mind you, but they probably do exist. In books. By men.

The Norman Conquests

April 13

Thomas Jefferson
(b. 1743 - d. July 4, 1826)
United States President

Whenever you are to do a thing, though it can never be known but to yourself, ask yourself how you would act were all the world looking at you, and act accordingly.

Letter of August 19, 1785

April 14

Anne Sullivan
(b. 1866 - d. October 20, 1936)
American Educator

No matter what happens, keep on beginning and failing. Each time you fail, start all over again, and you will grow stronger until you find that you have accomplished a purpose — not the one you began with perhaps, but one you will be glad to remember.

Quoted by Helen Keller

April 15

Leonardo da Vinci
(b. 1452 - d. May 2, 1519)
Florentine Artist

While I thought that I was learning how to live, I have been learning how to die.

Notebooks

April 16

Anatole France
(b. 1844 - d. October 13, 1924)
French Writer

That which cannot be avoided ought not to be punished.

Crainquebelle

April 17

David Grayson
(b. 1870 - d. July 12, 1946)
American Writer

Looking back, I have this to regret, that too often when I loved, I did not say so.

Under My Elm

April 18

Clarence Darrow
(b. 1857 - d. March 13, 1938)
American Lawyer

...every human being's life in this world is inevitably mixed with every other life and, no matter what laws we pass, no matter what precautions we take, unless the people we meet are kindly and decent and human and liberty-loving, then there is no liberty. Freedom comes from human beings, rather than from laws and institutions.

Speech of May 19, 1926

April 19

Henri Poincare
(b. 1854 - d. July 17, 1912)
French Mathematician

There are persons who consider the right to be ungrateful as the most precious of all liberties.

"Ethics and Science"

Henri Poincare

April 20

Paul Hazard
(b. 1878 - d. April 13, 1944)
French Historian

One man finds amusement in ambition, another in money-making, another in that altogether preposterous thing they call love. Little things amuse little minds. Great ones find amusement in trying to cover themselves with glory. As for myself, I find entertainment in the reflection that the whole business is just a way of passing the time, just another game.

The European Mind

April 21

Josh Billings
(b. 1818 - d. October 14, 1885)
American Humorist

It is better to give a man two thirds of the road than to quarrel with him, but to give him the whole is as much an insult to him as to yourself.

Uncle Sam's Uncle Josh

April 22

Madame de Stael
(b. 1766 - d. July 14, 1817)
French Writer

When one does not know how to convince, one oppresses; in all power relations among governors and governed, as ability declines, usurpation increases.

"Literature Considered in its Relation to Social Institutes"

April 23

William Shakespeare
(b. 1564 - d. April 23, 1616)
English Dramatist

If you'll be patient, I'll no more be mad;
That cures us both.

Cymbeline, II

April 24

Shirley MacLaine
(b. 1934 -   )
American Actress

The more I traveled the more I realized that fear makes strangers of people who should be friends.

Don't Fall Off the Mountain

April 25

Edward R. Murrow
(b. 1908 - d. April 27, 1965)
American Broadcaster

I would like television to produce some itching pills, rather than this endless outpouring of tranquilizers.

Speech of October 15, 1958

April 26

Marcus Aurelius
(b. 121 - d. March 17, 180)
Roman Emperor

Often have I marvelled how each one of us loves himself above all men, yet sets less store by his own opinion of himself than by that of everyone else.

Meditations

April 27

Maurice Baring
(b. 1874 - d. December 14, 1945)
English Journalist

If you would know what the Lord God thinks of money, you have only to look at those to whom he gives it.

Quoted by Dorothy Parker

April 28

Harper Lee
(b. 1926 -   )
American Novelist

When a child asks you something, answer him, for goodness' sake. But don't make a production of it. Children are children, but they can spot an evasion quicker than adults, and evasion simply muddles 'em.

To Kill a Mockingbird

April 29

William Randolph Hearst
(b. 1863 - d. August 14, 1951)
American Publisher

Any man who has the brains to think and the nerve to act for the benefit of the people of the country is considered a radical by those who are content with stagnation and willing to endure disaster.

Editorial of October 24, 1932

April 30

Annie Dillard
(b. 1945 -   )
American Writer

Cruelty is a mystery, and the waste of pain.

Pilgrim at Tinker Creek

May's coming, and high time it is.
Hal Borland

May 1

Ignazio Silone
(b. 1900 -   )
Italian Politician and Editor

Everyone of us is given the gift of life, and what a strange gift it is. If it is preserved jealously and self-ishly it impoverishes and saddens, but if it is spent for others it enriches and beautifies.

Quoted by Bernard Mandelbaum

May 2

Benjamin Spock
(b. 1903 -   )
American Pediatrician

Nothing shows more clearly America's reverence for money-making and mistrust of culture than the handing over of all the air waves to oily peddlers who sell hair dyes by wrapping them in stories of sentimentality or brutality, designed to appeal to the lowest levels of taste. It is as irresponsible as if all the universities and schools were turned over to advertisers with the right to choose the teachers, prescribed the content of courses, and interrupt the class every five minutes for another salesman.

Decent and Indecent

May 3

May Sarton
(b. 1912 -   )
American Poet and Writer

...if one does not have wild dreams of achievement, there is no spur even to get the dishes washed. One must think like a hero to behave like a merely decent human being.

Journal of a Solitude

May 4

Thomas Huxley
(b. 1825 - d. June 29, 1895)
English Biologist

There is a well-worn adage that those who set out upon a great enterprise would do well to count the cost. I am not sure that this is always true. I think that some of the very greatest enterprises in this world have been carried out successfully simply because the people who undertook them did not count the cost....

"Science and Education"

May 5

Soren Kierkegaard
(b. 1813 - d. November 11, 1855)
Danish Philosopher

The unhappy person is one who has his ideal, the content of his' life, the fullness of his consciousness, the essence of his being, in some manner outside of himself.

Either / Or

May 6

Joseph Joubert
(b. 1754 - d. May 4, 1824)
French Moralist

Only choose in marriage a woman whom you would choose as a friend if she were a man.

Pensees

May 7

Archibald MacLeish
(b. 1892 -   )
American Poet

...the fundamental truth of Jesus is that he does move love into the center of the human experience.

Interview with Bill Moyer

May 8

Harry Truman
(b. 1884 - d. December 26, 1972)
United States President

I do not like to hunt animals, and I never have. I do not believe in shooting at anything that cannot shoot back.

Give 'Em Hell Harry

May 9

James Barrie
(b. 1860 - d. June 19, 1937)
Scottish Novelist and Playwright

I'm not young enough to know everything.

The Admirable Crichton

May 10

Arthur Kopit
(b. 1937 -   )
American Playwright

...keeping people happy is *far* more difficult than either keeping them solvent, or keeping them alive.

The Day the Whores Came Out to Play Tennis

May 11

Mort Sahl
(b. 1927 -   )
American Entertainer

It is harder to live for your country than to die for it.

Interview with Pierre Berton

May 12

Theodor Reik
(b. 1888 - d. December 31, 1969)
Austrian/American Psychoanalist

A man who achieved something extraordinary in science or arts, will first encounter the antagonism and the animosity of the rabble, which often includes very educated people. No great man who was in advance of his time has escaped this destiny. He need not worry "how to make enemies"; his achievement itself will supply them.

Fragment of a Great Confession

May 13

Alphonse Daudet
(b. 1840 - d. December 16, 1897)
French Novelist

That person who is able by an effort of his mind to reconstruct a scene from life, hear the sounds and see the colors and gestures of it, and recall the odors, that man would do well to abstain from any wrong act.

Quoted by Leon Daudet

May 14

Hal Borland
(b. 1900 - d. February 22, 1978)
American Journalist

There are no limits to either time or distance, except as man himself may make them. I have but to touch the wind to know these things.

An American Year

May 15

Clifton Fadiman
(b. 1904 -   )
American Writer and Editor

When you reread a classic you do not see more in the book than you did before; you see more in *you* than there was before.

Any Number Can Play

May 16

Edward T. Hall
(b. 1914 -   )
American Anthropologist

...how man evolved with such an incredible reservoir of talent and such fantastic diversity is not completely understood. Man is not anywhere nearly enough in awe of himself, possibly because he knows so little and has nothing to measure himself against.

Beyond Culture

May 17

Henri Barbusse
(b. 1873 - d. August 30, 1935)
French Writer

Justice should be as cold as steel....Justice is not a virtue, as its name seems to indicate. It is an organization the virtue of which is to be feelingless. It does not aim at expiation. Its function is to establish warning example, to make of the criminal a thing to frighten off others.

The Inferno

May 18

Bertrand Russell
(b. 1872 - d. August 2, 1970)
British Philosopher

If one man offers you democracy and another offers you a bag of grain, at what stage of starvation will you prefer the grain to the vote?

Nobel Prize Acceptance Speech

May 19

Malcolm X
(b. 1925 - d. February 21, 1965)
American Black Nationalist Leader

Mankind's history has proven from one era to another that the true criterion of leadership is spiritual. Men are attracted by spirit. By power, men are forced. Love is engendered by spirit. By power, anxieties are created.

The Autobiography of Malcolm X

May 20

John Stuart Mill
(b. 1806 - d. May 8, 1873)
English Economist

That so few now dare to be eccentric, marks the chief danger of the time.

On Liberty

May 21

Alexander Pope
(b. 1688 - d. May 30, 1744)
English Poet

All Nature is but Art, unknown to thee;
All Chance, Direction, which thou canst not see;
All Discord, Harmony not understood;
All partial Evil, universal Good:
All, spite of Pride, in erring Reason's spite,
One truth is clear, WHATEVER IS, IS RIGHT.

An Essay on Man

May 22

Gerard de Nerval
(b. 1808 - d. January 25, 1855)
French Poet

The hour of our birth, the exact place on earth where
we appear, the first movement, the name, the room,
and all the consecrations and rituals imposed upon us,
establishes a lucky or unlucky series on which the whole
of our future hangs.

Selected Writings of Gerard de Nerval

May 23

Margaret Fuller
(b. 1810 - d. July 19, 1850)
American Writer

Children should not cull the fruits of reflection and observation early, but expand in the sun, and let thoughts come to them. They should not through books antedate their actual experiences, but should take them gradually, as sympathy and interpretation are needed. With me, much of life was devoured in the bud.

Memoirs

May 24

Harry Emerson Fosdick
(b. 1878 - d. October 5, 1969)
American Clergyman

Once when Ole Bull, the great violinist, was giving a concert in Paris, his A string snapped and he transposed the composition, and finished it on three strings. That is life — to have your A string snap and finish on three strings.

Riverside Sermons

May 25

Ralph Waldo Emerson
(b. 1803 - d. April 27, 1882)
American Philosopher and Poet

Open the doors of opportunity to talent and virtue and they do themselves justice, and property will not be in bad hands. In a free and just commonwealth, property rushes from the idle and imbecile to the industrious, brave and persevering.

Speech of 1868

May 26

Leonard Bacon
(b. 1887 - d. January 1, 1954)
American Poet

There never was a time when fire and music could not remold a universe no matter how shattered.

Semi-Centennial

May 27

Herman Wouk
(b. 1915 -   )
American Writer

You can't understand command till you've had it. It's the loneliest, most oppressive job in the whole world. It's a nightmare, unless you're an ox. You're forever teetering along a tiny path of correct decisions and good luck that meanders through an infinite gloom of possible mistakes.

The Caine Mutiny

May 28

Louis Agassiz
(b. 1807 - d. December 12, 1873)
Swiss/American Naturalist

I cannot afford to waste my time making money.

Quoted by William James

May 29

John F. Kennedy
(b. 1917 - d. November 22, 1963)
United States President

If we make peaceful revolution impossible, we make violent revolution inevitable.

Address of March 31, 1962

May 30

Mikhail Bakunin
(b. 1814 - d. July 1, 1876)
Russian Anarchist

Man becomes accustomed to anything, even fear.

Quoted by E.H. Carr

May 31

Walt Whitman
(b. 1819 - d. March 26, 1892)
American Poet

My final merit I refuse you, I refuse putting
 from me what I really *am,*
Encompass worlds, but never try to
 encompass *me,*
I crowd your sleekest and best by simply
 looking toward you.

"Song of Myself"

No price is set on the lavish summer;
June may be had by the poorest comer.
James Russell Lowell

June 1

James Graham
(b. 1792 - d. October 25, 1861)
English Statesman

Remember that when you're in the right you can afford
to keep your temper and that when you're in the wrong
you can't afford to lose it.

Treasury of the Art of Living

June 2

Ralph Friedman
(b. 1916 -)
American Writer

A radical says, "You can't have an omelette without breaking the eggs." A liberal says, "What's wrong with oatmeal?"

Ralph Friedman, Conversationally at Large

June 3

Sydney Smith
(b. 1771 - d. February 22, 1845)
English Clergyman

Mankind are always happier for having been happy; so that if you make them happy now, you make them happy twenty years hence, by the memory of it.

Wit and Wisdom of Sydney Smith

June 4

Charles Collingwood
(b. 1917 -   )
American Journalist and Novelist

Funny how men who have been in a war together always get nostalgic about it, no matter how miserable they had been, telling each other the same old anecdotes over and over again. I wondered whether twenty years from now middle-aged men would find themselves happily reminiscing over Vietnam.

The Defector

June 5

Max Friedlander
(b. 1867 - d. October 11, 1958)
American Art Critic

That mankind can endure with wars is proved; that it could endure without wars is not and cannot be proved.

Reminiscences and Reflections

June 6

William Ralph Inge
(b. 1860 - d. February 26, 1954)
English Clergyman

Whatever may be truly said about the good sense of a democracy during a great crisis, at ordinary times it does not bring the best men to the top.

Wit and Wisdom of Dean Inge

June 7

Nikki Giovanni
(b. 1943 -   )
American Poet

...it takes up so much energy just to keep yourself happy.

A Dialogue

June 8

Frank Lloyd Wright
(b. 1869 - d. April 9, 1959)
American Architect

An expert? Generally, a man who has stopped thinking because he knows!

A Testament

June 9

Samuel Nathaniel Behrman
(b. 1893 - d. September 9, 1973)
American Playwright

You speak of the anonymous dead. They're not anonymous. They're figures in the tapestry in which we ourselves are figures. They've given us what we are. When you're young, you try to get away from them. But when you're mature, you return to them. You'll embrace them, and they'll support you, I promise you. Every breath you draw — every thought you have — every note you set down — you're living off them.

The Cold Wind and the Warm

June 10

Saul Bellow
(b. 1915 -)
Canadian/American Novelist

I couldn't help feeling sympathetic....But my attitude is that if people are going to undo themselves before you, you shouldn't do them up again. You should let them retie their own parcels.

Henderson the Rain King

June 11

Alexander Bain
(b. 1818 - d. September 18, 1903)
British Philosopher

Encourage a man to say whatever he thinks, and you make the most of him; for difficult questions, where the mind needs all its powers, there should be no burdensome 'caution' in giving out the results.

Practical Essays

June 12

Anne Frank
(b. 1929 - d. 1945)
German/Dutch Diarist

I keep my ideals, because in spite of everything I still
believe that people are really good at heart.

Diary of Anne Frank

June 13

William Butler Yeats
(b. 1865 - d. January 28, 1939)
Irish Poet and Playwright

Science, separated from philosophy, is the opium of the suburbs.

Explorations

June 14

Harriet Beecher Stowe
(b. 1811 - d. July 1, 1896)
American Educator and Writer

...the ear that has never heard anything but abuse is strangely incredulous of anything so heavenly as kindness....

Uncle Tom's Cabin

June 15

Thaddeus Golas
(b. 1926 -   )
American Writer

It is not a personal affront to you when someone is being discordant, it is a measure of his pain. He's showing you how much he hurts, and how much compassion he needs.

The Lazy Man's Guide to Enlightenment

June 16

Adam Smith
(b. 1723 - d. July 17, 1790)
Scottish Economic Philosopher

The real price of every thing, what every thing really costs to the man who wants to acquire it, is the toil and trouble of acquiring it.

Wealth of Nations

June 17

John Hersey
(b. 1914 -   )
American Novelist

Why do you keep silent about the reason for war? At least, what *I* think is the reason for war: that some men enjoy it , some men enjoy it too much.

The War Lover

June 18

Philip Barry
(b. 1896 - d. December 3,1949)
American Playwright

I have found out a simple thing: that in existence there are three estates. There is this life of chairs and tables, of getting up and sitting down. There is the life one lives in one's imagining, in which one wishes, dreams, remembers. There is the life past death, which in itself contains the others. The three estates are one. We dwell now in this one, now in that — but in whichever we may be, breezes from the others still blow upon us.

The Hotel Universe

June 19

Blaise Pascal
(b. 1623 - d. August 19, 1662)
French Scientist

Children are astonished to see their comrades respected.

Pensees

June 20

Lillian Hellman
(b. 1905 -   )
American Playwright

I don't like to talk about convictions. I'm never sure I'm telling the truth.

Scoundrel Time

June 21

Jean Paul Sartre
(b. 1905 -   )
French Writer and Philosopher

Every man has his natural place; its altitude is determined by neither pride nor value: childhood decides. Mine is a sixth floor in Paris with a view overlooking the roofs.

The Words

June 22

Anne Morrow Lindbergh
(b. 1906 -   )
American Writer

When you love someone you do not love them all the time, in exactly the same way, from moment to moment. It is an impossibility. It is even a lie to pretend to. And yet this is exactly what most of us demand.

Gift from the Sea

June 23

Irvin S. Cobb
(b. 1876 - d. March 10, 1944)
American Journalist

...why should one practice what he preaches so long as he can enjoy the virtuous satisfaction of having preached — and find other people who are so weak-willed as to do the practicing?

Exit Laughing

June 24

Henry Ward Beecher
(b. 1813 - d. March 8, 1887)
American Clergyman

Christian men should use refinement on this principle: the more I have, the more I owe to those who have less than I.

Quoted by Theodore Parker

June 25

George Orwell
(b. 1903 - d. January 21, 1950)
British Writer

The rich and the poor are differentiated by their incomes and nothing else, and the average millionaire is only the average dishwasher dressed in a new suit. Everyone who has mixed in equal terms with the poor knows this quite well.

Down and Out in Paris and London

June 26

Pearl S. Buck
(b. 1892 - d. March 6, 1973)
American Novelist

Whenever I hear a woman whose conversation is altogether of what her children do and say I feel sorry for those children. How can they go out and live happily in a world of which they are not the center? It is a bad thing for anybody at any time in his life to feel that he is the center of any world. Home ought to be a living unit in a living world, and not a hole into which to crawl to escape the realities of life.

"At Home in the World"

Helen Keller
June 27

June 27

Helen Keller
(b. 1880 - d. June 1, 1968)
American Author and Educator

It seems to me that there is in each of us a capacity to comprehend the impressions and emotions which have been experienced by mankind from the beginning. Each individual has a subconscious memory of the green earth and murmuring waters, and blindness and deafness cannot rob him of this gift from past generations. This inherited capacity is a sort of sixth sense — a soul-sense which sees, hears, feels, all in one.

The Story of My Life

June 28

Ashley Montagu
(b. 1905 -   )
American Anthropologist

When people don't act upon the knowledge they possess it can mean only one thing: *they don't really believe it.*

On Being Intelligent

June 29

Antoine de Saint-Exupery
(b. 1900 - d. July 31, 1944)
French Aviator and Writer

"Men have forgotten this truth," said the fox. "But you must not forget it. You become responsible, forever, for what you have tamed."

The Little Prince

June 30

Georges Duhamel
(b. 1884 - d. April 13, 1966)
French Writer

"Liberty...lies, not in institutions, but in the sensation of freedom that we derive from them. We are the freest people on earth."
"I know. But wait a moment. I have in my pocket several of your small coins on which is stamped the word 'Liberty'. And what do you see immediately under that word? The figure of a buffalo or an Indian. Oh, Irony! They represent two free and spirited races that you have destroyed in less that three centuries."

America the Menace

July 1

George Sand
(b. 1804 - d. June 8, 1876)
French Novelist

I would like little ones to be shown only the sweet and the good of life, until the time when reason can help them to accept or to fight the bad.

Letter of February 24, 1869

July 2

Hermann Hesse
(b. 1877 - d. August 9, 1962)
German Novelist and Poet

To live in the world as though it were not the world, to observe the law and yet to be above it, to possess "as though one did not possess," to renounce as though no renunciation were involved — only humor is able to live up to these revered and often formulated demands of a noble philosophy of life.

Reflections

July 3

Franz Kafka
(b. 1883 - d. June 3, 1924)
Czech Writer

You don't have to leave the house. Remain at your table and listen. Don't even listen, just wait. Don't even wait, be absolutely silent and alone. The world will come to you and let you take off its mask, it can't refuse.

Kafka: The Torment of Man

July 4

Nathaniel Hawthorne
(b. 1804 - d. May 19,1864)
American Writer

Caresses, expressions of one sort or another, are necessary to the life of the affections, as leaves are to the life of a tree. If they are wholly restrained, love will die at the roots.

American Notebooks

July 5

George Borrow
(b. 1803 - d. July 26,1881)
English Linguist

What is the use of having money unless you let people know you have it?

Lavengro

July 6

Eleanor Clark
(b. 1913 -   )
American Writer

We can't make God a reality if He isn't one, nor apparently prove it if He is.   But we *can* make an illusion of noble spaces.

Baldur's Gate

July 7

Gustav Mahler
(b. 1860 - d. May 18, 1911)
Austrian Composer

The important thing is never to let oneself be guided by the opinion of one's contemporaries and, in both one's life and one's work, to continue steadfastly on one's way without letting oneself be either defeated by failure or diverted by applause.

Letter of March 1901

Gustav Mahler

July 8

Fritz Perls
(b. 1894 - d. March 14, 1970)
German/American Psychotherapist

Many people dedicate their lives to actualize a concept of what they *should* be like, rather than to actualize *themselves*. This difference between *self*-actualizing and self-*image* actualizing is *very* important. Most people only live for their image. Where some people have a self, most people have a void, because they are so busy projecting themselves as this or that. This is again the curse of the ideal. The curse that you should not be what you are.

Gestalt Therapy Verbatim

July 9

Ernest Dimnet
(b. 1866 - d. December 8, 1954)
French Cleric

...how can I forget the long slow years in which my soul ripened in peace in its closed garden? Probably each one of us has his own old world, that is to say, the time when he was less conscious of reacting upon his surroundings than of being nurtured by them. The recollection of that time is our individual poetry.

My Old World

July 10

Marcel Proust
(b. 1871 - d. November 18, 1922)
French Novelist

Let us leave pretty women to men devoid of imagination.

The Sweet Cheat Gone

July 11

Leon Bloy
(b. 1846 - d. November 3, 1917)
French Writer

The worst evil is not committing crimes but failing to do the good one could do. It is the sin of *omission,* which is nothing other than non-love, and of which no man accuses himself.

Pilgrim of the Absolute

July 12

Henry David Thoreau
(b. 1817 - d. May 6, 1862)
American Writer and Philosopher

It is something to be able to paint a particular picture, or to carve a statue, and so to make a few objects beautiful; but it is far more glorious to carve and paint the very atmosphere and medium through which we look, which morally we can do. To affect the quality of the day, that is the highest of the arts.

Walden

July 13

Gustav Freytag
(b. 1816 - d. April 30, 1895)
German Novelist and Playwright

Not every age allows its sons to reap the results which remain great for all time, and...not every century is fitted to make the men who live in it distinguished and happy.

The Journalists

July 14

Ingmar Bergman
(b. 1918 -   )
Swedish Film Writer and Director

...it is my opinion that art lost its basic creative drive the moment it was separated from worship....In former days the artist remained unknown and his work was to the glory of God. He lived and died without being more or less important than other artisans; 'eternal values', 'immortality', and 'masterpiece' were terms not applicable in his case....The ability to create was a gift. In such a world flourished invulnerable assurance and natural humility.

Introduction to *The Seventh Seal*

July 15

Walter Benjamin
(b. 1892 - d. September 26, 1940)
German Philosopher

It is only for the sake of those without hope that hope is given to us.

"Goethe"

July 16

Mary Baker Eddy
(b. 1821 - d. December 3, 1910)
American Religious Leader

Stand porter at the door of thought. Admitting only such conclusions as you wish realized in bodily results, you will control yourself harmoniously.

Science and Health

July 17

Hannah Senesh
(b. 1921 - d. November 7, 1944)
Jewish Patriot

...does one have the right to long for what is distant, and give up what is close at hand?

Diary

July 18

S.I. Hayakawa
(b. 1906 -)
American Educator and Senator

What happens in the schools is not unlike what happens in society at large when the penalties of improvidence, laziness, or ignorance are not just softened, but removed. When there is no such thing as failure, there is no such thing as success either.

Harper's Magazine, January 1978

July 19

Edgar Degas
(b. 1834 - d. September 26, 1917)
French Painter

Leisure is the loveliest thing in the world when one doesn't suffer from it.

Quoted by Daniel Halevy

July 20

Hermann Keyserling
(b. 1880 - d. April 26, 1946)
German Philosopher

All nations are, of course, thoroughly unpleasant things. Man, as such, is a dubious enough sort of creature; the moment he emerges as a collectivity, the objectionable side of him increases in direct proportion as the pleasant side dwindles....

Europe

July 21

Ernest Hemingway
(b. 1898 - d. July 2, 1961)
American Novelist

...about morals, I know only what is moral is what you feel good after and what is immoral is what you feel bad after.

Death in the Afternoon

July 22

Edward Dahlberg
(b. 1900 - d. February 27, 1977)
American Writer

A man without appetite cannot be called virtuous because he does not rule desires that never molest him.

The Sorrows of Priapus

July 23

Salvador de Madariaga
(b. 1886 -   )
Spanish Diplomat and Writer

...our problems are not here for us to solve them but for them to solve us.

Morning Without Noon

July 24

Amelia Earhart
(b. 1897 - d. July 1937)
American Aviator

It seems to me that the effect of having other interests beyond those exclusively domestic works well. The more one does and sees and feels, the more one is able to do, and the more genuine may be one's appreciation of fundamental things like home, and love and understanding companionship.

Soaring Wings

July 25

Eric Hoffer
(b. 1902 -   )
American Writer

The remarkable thing is that we really love our neighbor as ourselves; we do unto others as we do unto ourselves. We hate others as we hate ourselves. We are tolerant toward others when we tolerate ourselves. We forgive others when we forgive ourselves....It is not love of self but hatred of self which is at the root of the troubles that afflict our world.

The Passionate State of Mind

July 26

George Bernard Shaw
(b. 1856 - d. November 2, 1950)
British Dramatist

The reasonable man adapts himself to the world: the unreasonable one persists in trying to adapt the world to himself. Therefore all progress depends on the unreasonable man.

Man and Superman

July 27

Hillaire Belloc
(b. 1870 - d. July 16, 1953)
English Writer

Save on the rare occasions when the Sun is shining, I am only here for fun.

"On the Same"

July 28

Marcel Duchamp
(b. 1887 - d. October 1, 1968)
French/American Artist

Don't swallow up bits of other people; it digests badly and gets noticed.

Quoted by H.P. Roche

July 29

Dag Hammarskjold
(b. 1905 - d. September 18, 1961)
Swedish Statesman

We are not permitted to choose the frame of our destiny. But what we put into it is ours. He who wills adventure will experience it — according to the measure of his courage. He who wills sacrifice will be sacrificed — according to the measure of his purity of heart.

Markings

July 30

Emily Bronte
(b. 1818 - d. December 18, 1848)
English Novelist and Poet

...treachery and violence are spears pointed at both ends: they wound those who resort to them worse than their enemies.

Wuthering Heights

July 31

Lynn Reid Banks
(b. 1929 -   )
English Novelist

I think those under thirty find it difficult to accept
the fact that some actions may have results that are
final and inescapable. When you're young, everything
seems reversible, remittable. Time will put everything
right. Unkind words, ill-judged behavior, stupidity,
cruelty — it can all be made up for, cancelled out
later.

The L-Shaped Room

August 1

Herman Melville
(b. 1819 - d. September 28, 1891)
American Novelist

...it is better to fail in originality than to succeed in imitation. He who has never failed somewhere, that man can not be great. Failure is the true test of greatness. And if it be said that continual success is a proof that a man wisely knows his powers, it is only to be added that, in that case, he knows them to be small.

"Hawthorne and His Moses"

August 2

James Baldwin
(b. 1924 -   )
American Writer

To defend oneself against a fear is simply to insure that one will, one day, be conquered by it; fears must be faced.

The Fire Next Time

August 3

Isabelle Caroline Somerset
(b. 1851 - d. March 12,1921)
English Philanthropist

This life is such a tiny part of a great whole, we cannot hope to solve the riddle of life. We must never think we cannot hold two inconsistent views.

Diary

August 4

Percy Bysshe Shelley
(b. 1792 - d. July 8, 1822)
English Poet

We look before and after,
    And pine for what is not;
Our sincerest laughter
    With some pain is fraught;
Our sweetest songs are those that tell of saddest thought.

"To a Skylark"

August 5

Wendell Berry
(b. 1943 -   )
American Educator and Poet

...it is not the life that is fittest (by which we have meant the most violent) that survives, but rather the life that is most decent — the life that is most generous and wise in its relation to the earth.

A Continuous Harmony

August 6

Alfred Lord Tennyson
(b. 1809 - d. October 6, 1892)
English Poet

'Tis better to have loved and lost than never to have loved at all.

In Memoriam

August 7

Alice James
(b. 1848 - d. March 5, 1892)
American Diarist

The only thing which survives is the resistance we bring to life, and not the strain life brings to us.

Diary

August 8

Sara Teasdale
(b. 1884 - d. January 29, 1933)
American Poet

No one worth possessing
Can be quite possessed.

"Advice to a Girl"

August 9

Jennifer Froistad
(b. 1940 -   )
American Educational Administrator

Afraid to reach and frightened of touch,
We pass each other in a noisy rush.
Never meeting another's eyes
Never seeing where beauty lies.

Our talk of love and brotherhood
Are simply words too often heard.
We'll never know what either means
Till our walls come down and we are seen.

"Song of the Great Round Earth"

August 10

Camillo Cavour
(b. 1810 - d. June 6, 1861)
Italian Statesman

In all the relations of life, in all countries of the world,
it is with the oppressed that it is necessary to live:
those who are happy and powerful are ignorant of
half the feelings and ideas of mankind.

Diary

August 11

Robert Ingersoll
(b. 1833 - d. July 21, 1899)
American Lawyer

...if you wish to reflect credit on your father and mother, do it by accomplishing more than they did, because you live in a better time.

Mistakes of Moses

August 12

Robert Southey
(b. 1774 - d. March 21, 1843)
English Poet

All men, even the vicious themselves, know that wickedness leads to misery; but many even among the good and the wise, have yet to learn that misery is almost as often the cause of wickedness.

Colloquies on Society

August 13

Lucy Stone
(b. 1818 - d. October 18, 1893)
American Reformer

The politician is the creature of the public sentiment —
never goes ahead of it because he depends on it....To
make the public sentiment, on the side of all that is
just and true and noble, is the highest use of life.

Morning Star

August 14

John Galsworthy
(b. 1867 - d. January 31, 1933)
English Novelist and Playwright

"It's only," said H, "when men run in packs that
they lose their sense of decency. At least that's my
experience. Individual man...is more given to generosity
than meanness, rarely brutal, inclines in fact to be a
gentleman. It's when you add three or four more to
him that his sense of decency, his sense of personal
responsibility, his private standards, go by the board."

"The Pack"

August 15

Sir Walter Scott
(b. 1771 - d. September 21, 1832)
Scottish Poet and Novelist

Can not may be a more civil phrase than *will not,* but the expressions are synonymous where there is no moral responsibility.

Rob Roy

August 16

Eli Siegel
(b. 1902 -   )
American Poet

The way we are vexed ought to be improving constantly.

Damned Welcome

August 17

Jean de La Bruyere
(b. 1645 - d. May 10, 1696)
French Philosopher

Women exceed the generality of men in Love, but men have the advantage in Friendship.

Characters

August 18

Brian W. Aldiss
(b. 1925 -   )
British Novelist

In a few generations, all mankind will be vegetarian.... Once it is generally realized that the animals are such close kin to us, then meat-eating will be disdained as too near to canibalism for comfort. Can you imagine what a civilizing effect that will have on the multitude?

Frankenstein Unbound

August 19

Gabrielle (Coco) Chanel
(b. 1883 - d. January 10, 1971)
French Fashion Designer

Success is often achieved by those who don't know that failure is inevitable.

McCall's Magazine

August 20

Paul Tillich
(b. 1886 - d. October 22, 1965)
German/American Theologian

The courage to be is rooted in the God who appears when God has disappeared in the anxiety of doubt.

The Courage to Be

August 21

Melvin Van Peebles
(b. 1932 -   )
American Writer

Maybe each heart is given the same amount of emotions for a lifetime regardless of the circumstances; so much hate and pity, love and fear per person...and if the heart doesn't have bullets, or third movements, or escapes, to worry about it settles for hair dyes and football pools.

A Bear for the F.B.I.

August 22

Max Scheler
(b. 1874 - d. May 19,1928)
German Philosopher

I only point the way; a sign doesn't have to go where it points.

Phenomenology of Community

August 23

Edgar Lee Masters
(b. 1869 - d. March 5, 1950)
English Poet

Immortality is not a gift,
Immortality is an achievement;
And only those who strive mightily
Shall possess it.

"The Village Atheist"

August 24

Milton Mayer
(b. 1908 -   )
American Educator and Author

The young respect the old because the old are old. If
the old are young, they are not respected by the young
(who have no need to respect one another.) And if
the old pretend to be young, they are pretending not
to be respectable and don't want to be respected.

If Men Were Angels

August 25

Walt Kelly
(b. 1913 - d. October 18, 1973)
American Cartoonist

Resolve, then, that on this very ground, with small flags waving and tinny blasts on tiny trumpets, we shall meet the enemy, and not only may he be ours, he may be us.

"Pogo"

August 26

Henry Chester Tracy
(b. 1876 - d. December 19, 1958)
American Essayist

By some deep law of our being we are obliged to assume an attitude...and make it good.

American Naturists

August 27

Lloyd C. Douglas
(b. 1877 - d. February 13, 1951)
American Novelist

There isn't so very much difference, after all, between the height of stumbling blocks and stepping stones. Whether they are to serve as something to climb up over or fall down over depends upon our own mood as we approach them.

The Living Faith

August 28

Johann Wolfgang von Goethe
(b. 1749 - d. March 22, 1832)
German Poet

All excellent things oppress us for a moment because we do not feel equal to them; only if we subsequently assimilate them, joining them to our own intellectual and emotional energies, shall we love and value them.

''Proverbs in Prose''

August 29

Oliver Wendell Holmes
(b. 1809 - d. October 7, 1894)
American Physician and Poet

When one has had *all* his conceit taken out of him, when he has lost *all* his illusions, his feathers will soon soak through, and he will fly no more.

Autocrat at the Breakfast Table

August 30

Mary Shelley
(b. 1797 - d. February 1, 1851)
English Writer

Learn from me, if not by my precepts, at least by my example, how dangerous is the acquirement of knowledge, and how much happier that man is who believes his native town to be the world, than he who aspires to become greater than his nature will allow.

Frankenstein

August 31

Maria Montessori
(b. 1870 - d. May 6, 1952)
Italian Physician and Educator

If survival depended solely on the triumph of the strong then the species would perish. So the real reason for survival, the principle factor in the "struggle of existence", is the *love of adults* for their young.

The Absorbent Mind

September 1

Edgar Rice Burroughs
(b. 1875 - d. March 19, 1950)
American Novelist

"We are what we are born," rejoined Gemnon; "some are beasts, some are men, and some are men who behave like beasts."

"But none, thank God, are beasts that behave like men," retorted Tarzan, smiling.

The City of Gold

September 2

Newell D. Hillis
(b. 1858 - d. February 25, 1929)
American Clergyman

An age fruitful in foolish and false ideas has produced none more erroneous than the idea that labour has produced all wealth.

The Fortune of the Republic

September 3

Helen Blumenstiel
(b. 1899 - d. March 25, 1975)
American Artist and Educator

To have been born seems to me something to celebrate and to be alive and aware seems the greatest gift one could be given. Since we're indebted to our parents for this gift, celebrating one's birthday is, in a manner of speaking, paying homage to them.

Letter of 1964

September 4

Richard Wright
(b. 1908 - d. November 28, 1960)
American Novelist

The truth is that our world — a world for all men,
black, brown, yellow, and white — will either be all
rational or totally irrational. For better or worse, it
will eventually be one world.

White Man, Listen!

September 5

John Cage
(b. 1912 -   )
American Composer

When I had a Jaguar, I noticed anyone else who drove
a Jaguar.   Now I'm wearing jeans instead of suits,
I notice nearly everyone.

M - Writings '62-'72

September 6

Jane Addams
(b. 1860 - d. May 21, 1935)
American Social Reformer

The good we secure for ourselves is precarious and
uncertain until it is secured for all of us and incorporated
into our common life.

Twenty Years at Hull-House

September 7

W.N.P. Barbellion
(b. 1889 - d. October 22,1919)
English Biologist

Perhaps too great an enthusiasm exhausts the spirit. Love kills. I know it. The love of one's art or profession, passion for another's soul, for one's children, sap the life and blood and hurry us on to the grave...lust of knowledge is as fatal as any other kind.
  I know it. But I don't care.

Enjoying Life

September 8

John Locke
(b. 1632 - d. October 28,1704)
English Philosopher

New opinions are always suspected, and usually opposed, without any other reason but because they are not already common.

Essay on Human Understanding

September 9

Leo Tolstoy
(b. 1828 - d. November 20, 1910)
Russian Novelist

Refusals of military service in Christian states began when in Christian states military service appeared. Or rather when the states, the power of which rests upon violence, laid claim to Christianity without giving up violence. In truth, it cannot be otherwise. A Christian, whose doctrine enjoins upon him humility, non-resistance to evil, love to all (even to the most malicious), cannot be a soldier; that is, he cannot join a class of men whose business is to kill their fellow-men. Therefore it is that these Christians have always refused and now refuse military service.

But of true Christians there have always been but few.

"The Beginning of the End"

September 10

Arthur H. Compton
(b. 1892 - d. March 15, 1962)
American Physicist

Science has created a world in which Christianity is an imperative.

Quoted by Harry Emerson Fosdick

Leo Tolstoy

September 11

D.H. Lawrence
(b. 1885 - d. March 2, 1930)
English Novelist and Poet

Those that go searching for love
only make manifest their own lovelessness,
and the loveless never find love,
only the loving find love,
and they never have to seek for it.

"Search for Love"

September 12

H.L. Mencken
(b. 1880 - d. January 29, 1956)
American Editor and Humorist

The objection to Puritans is not that they try to make us think as they do, but that they try to make us do as they think.

The Young Mencken

September 13

J.B. Priestley
(b. 1894 -   )
English Writer

When the young behave badly, as we are told so many of them do now, it is because society has already behaved worse. We have the teenagers, like the politicians and the wars, that we deserve.

Margin Released

September 14

Sydney J. Harris
(b. 1917 -   )
American Journalist

Children never pick up the good habits from their playmates, but only the bad ones; for the same reason that health is not catching but disease is.

Last Things First

September 15

Francois de La Rochefoucauld
(b. 1613 - d. March 17, 1680)
French Writer

We forgive to the extent that we love.

The Maxims of La Rochefoucauld

September 16

Clive Bell
(b. 1881 - d. September 18, 1964)
English Art Critic

Those who take art seriously are those who find in art an escape from life. No wonder they take it seriously.

Enjoying Pictures

September 17

William Carlos Williams
(b. 1883 - d. March 4, 1963)
American Poet and Physician

Why pretend to remember the weather two years back?
Why not? Listen close then repeat after others what
they have just said and win a reputation for vivacity.
Oh feed upon petals of edelweiss! One dew drop, if
it be from the right flower, is five years' drink!

Imaginations

September 18

Samuel Johnson
(b. 1709 - d. December 13, 1784)
English Poet and Essayist

No man is obliged to do as much as he can do. A man
is to have part of his life to himself.

Boswell's Life of Johnson, volume I

September 19

William Golding
(b. 1911 -)
English Novelist

I devised a coherent system for living. It was a moral
system, which was wholly logical. Of course, as I
readily admitted, conversion of the world to my way of
thinking might be difficult, since my system did away
with a number of trifles, such as big business, centralized
government, armies, marriage....

"Thinking as a Hobby"

September 20

Elizabeth Kenny
(b. 1886 - d. November 30, 1952)
Australian Nurse

He who angers you conquers you.

Fifty Great Modern Lives

September 21

H.G. Wells
(b. 1866 - d. August 13, 1946)
English Novelist and Historian

We all need training, training in the balanced attitude.

Of everything we need to say THIS IS TRUE, BUT IT IS NOT QUITE TRUE.

Of everything we need to say, this is true in relation to things in or near its plane but not true of other things.

Of everything we have to remember, this may be truer for us than for other people.

First and Last Things

September 22

Lord Chesterfield
(b. 1694 - d. March 24, 1773)
English Statesman

Never seem wiser, nor more learned than the people you
are with.

Letter of February 22, 1748

September 23

Walter Lippmann
(b. 1889 - d. December 14, 1974)
American Editor and Writer

The emotion of love, in spite of the romantics, is not
self-sustaining; it endures only when the lovers love
many things together, and not merely each other.

A Preface of Morals

September 24

Florida Scott-Maxwell
(b. 1884 -   )
American Writer

...the pain that for me is inherent in life is that we do not know when we create and when we destroy. That is our incurable blindness, but perhaps we are less dangerous if we know we do not see.

The Measure of My Days

September 25

William Faulkner
(b. 1897 - d. July 6, 1962)
American Novelist

There is no such thing as *was* — only *is*. If *was* existed, there would be no grief or sorrow.

Writers at Work

September 26

Martin Heidegger
(b. 1889 - d. May 26, 1976)
German Philosopher

The greater the master, the more completely his person vanishes behind his work.

Discourse on Thinking

September 27

Henri Frederic Amiel
(b. 1821 - d. May 11, 1881)
Swiss Writer

Let mystery have its place in you; do not be always turning up your whole soil with the plowshare of self-examination, but leave a little fallow corner in your heart ready for any seed the winds may bring, and reserve a nook of shadow for the passing bird; keep a place in your heart for the unexpected guests, an altar for the unknown God.

Journals, December 2, 1851

September 28

Kate Wiggin
(b. 1856 - d. August 24, 1923)
American Writer and Educator

We do our hair alike, dress alike as much as possible, eat and drink alike, talk alike — I am not even sure that we do not think alike: and what will become of the poor world when we are all let loose upon it on the same day of June? Will life, real life, bring our true selves back to us? Will love and duty and sorrow and trouble and work finally wear off the "school stamp" that has been pressed upon all of us until we look like rows of shining copper cents fresh from the mint?

New Chronicles of Rebecca

September 29

Herbert Agar
(b. 1897 -   )
American Editor and Writer

All history shows that it is easier to confer power upon governments than to withdraw it. We must be jealous and vigilant to see that the power we are conferring by our votes is used for our own purposes, and that once those purposes are served the power is relinquished.

Pursuit of Happiness

September 30

Elie Wiesel
(b. 1928 -   )
Romanian/American Writer

Man walks the moon but his soul remains riveted to earth. Once upon a time it was the opposite.

Souls on Fire

Sycamore leaves on
the lawn jump in the rain, let
go of October.

William Stafford

October 1

Austin O'Malley
(b. 1858 - d. February 25, 1932)
American Physician and Writer

Memory is a crazy woman that hoards colored rags and throws away food.

Keystones of Thought

October 2

Mohandas K. Gandhi
(b. 1869 - d. January 30, 1948)
Indian Philosopher

My aim is not to be consistent with my previous state-
ments on a given question, but to be consistent with
truth as it may present itself to me at a given moment.
The result has been that I have grown from truth to
truth.

Harijan

October 3

Thomas Wolfe
(b. 1900 - d. September 15, 1938)
American Novelist

...the essence of belief is doubt, the essence of reality is questioning. The essence of Time is Flow, not Fix. The essence of faith is the knowledge that all flows and that everything must change. The growing man is Man-Alive, and his "philosophy" must grow, must flow, with him.

You Can't Go Home Again

October 4

Alvin Toffler
(b. 1928 -   )
American

If we do not learn from history, we shall be compelled to relive it. True. But if we do not change the future, we shall be compelled to endure it. And that could be worse.

The Futurists

October 5

Denis Diderot
(b. 1713 - d. July 30, 1784)
French Philosopher

...distrust him who wants to put order into things. To make order is always to make oneself the master of others by constraining them....

Philosophical Works

October 6

George Horace Lorimer
(b. 1867 - d. October 22, 1937)
American Editor

The boy who does anything just because the other fellows do it is apt to scratch a poor man's back all his life.

Letters to His Godson

October 7

Helen MacInnes
(b. 1907 -   )
Scottish/American Novelist

In the civilized world, evil and good are so often entwined round each other that the quickest way to end evil is to cut back both.

Decision at Delphi

October 8

John W. Gardner
(b. 1912 -   )
American Educator and Writer

The society which scorns excellence in plumbing because plumbing is a humble activity and tolerates shoddiness in philosophy because it is an exalted activity will have neither good plumbing nor good philosophy. Neither its pipes nor its theories will hold water.

Excellence

October 9

Miguel de Cervantes
(b. 1547 - d. April 23, 1616)
Spanish Novelist

Let the tears of the poor find more compassion, but not more justice, from you than the pleadings of the wealthy.

Don Quixote, volume II

October 10

Lin Yutang
(b. 1895 - d. March 26, 1976)
Chinese/American Writer

All I know is that if God loves me only half as much as my mother does, he will not send me to Hell.

The Importance of Living

October 11

Eleanor Roosevelt
(b. 1884 - d. November 7, 1962)
American Philanthropist and Diplomat

No one can make you feel inferior without your consent.

Catholic Digest, August 1960

October 12

Ann Petry
(b. 1912 -   )
American Novelist

He wondered if anyone, anywhere, any time, had looked forward to something, waited for it, dreamed over it, shaping and reshaping it in his mind, and then had found the reality exactly like the dream. He doubted it. Reality always ate the living heart out of a dream.

A Country Place

October 13

Vivian Murphy
(b. 1920 -   )
American Home Administrator

My father was the most gentle yet forceful man I've known, and he used to win most of the family arguments. At the height of his fury toward my mother he would shout, "Stop that, dearest, sweetheart, darling, dammit!"

Personal Conversation May 1978

October 14

E.E. Cummings
(b. 1894 - d. September 3, 1962)
American Poet

doubting can turn men's see to stare
their faith to how their joy to why
their stride and breathing to limp and prove.

"1 × 1"

October 15

Friedrich Nietzsche
(b. 1844 - d. August 25, 1900)
German Philosopher

Here the ways of men part: if you wish to strive for peace of soul and pleasure, then believe; if you wish to be a devotee of truth, then inquire....

Letter of June 11, 1865

October 16

Oscar Wilde
(b. 1854 - d. November 30, 1900)
Irish Poet and Dramatist

Good people do a great deal of harm in the world.
Certainly the greatest harm they do is that they make
badness of such extraordinary importance. It is absurd
to divide people into good and bad. People are either
charming or tedious.

Lady Windemere's Fan

October 17

Ihab Hassan
(b. 1925 -   )
American Educator and Writer

They used to say: the kingdom of the dead is larger
than any kingdom. But the earth has now exploded.
Soon the day may come when there will be more people
alive than ever lived.
   When the quick are more populous than all the
departed, will history reverse itself? End?

Paracriticisms

October 18

Logan Pearsall Smith
(b. 1865 - d. March 2, 1946)
English/American Writer

You cannot be both fashionable and first-rate.

All Trivia

October 19

Lewis Mumford
(b. 1895 -   )
American Writer and Historian

Each of us must ask himself: what portion of my life do I spend in the service of an idea and a purpose that will outlast this life and at the same time greatly fulfill it?

In the Name of Sanity

October 20

Wayne Morse
(b. 1900 - d. July 22, 1974)
American Senator

They're not free, those men in the Senate. A free man is a man who is free to do what he knows is right. They have to take party orders and do things for expediency. Once you put expediency above principle, there is no principle left.

Collier's Magazine April 4, 1953

October 21

Samuel Taylor Coleridge
(b. 1772 - d. July 25, 1834)
English Poet

Good and bad men are each less so than they seem.

Table Talk

October 22

Doris Lessing
(b. 1919 -   )
British Novelist

When a woman looks at a child she sees all the things he's been at the same time. When I look at Janet sometimes I see her as a small baby and I *feel* her inside my belly and I see her as various sizes of a small girl, all at the same time....That's how women see things. Everything in a sort of continuous creative stream....Well, isn't it natural we should?

The Golden Notebook

October 23

Allen Wheelis
(b. 1915 -   )
American Psychiatrist

To know the good is a dangerous thing; to know it for sure is usually fatal for somebody.

The Moralist

October 24

William Penn
(b. 1644 - d. July 30, 1718)
English Colonist

He that has more Knowledge than Judgment, is made for *another Man's* use more than his own.

Some Fruits of Solitude

October 25

Pablo Picasso
(b. 1881 - d. April 8, 1973)
Spanish Artist

...love must be proved by facts and not by reasons. What one does is what counts and not what one had the intentions of doing.

The Arts, May 1923

October 26

Gustav Eckstein
(b. 1890 -   )
American Physiologist and Writer

A tomato does not communicate with a tomato, we believe. We could be wrong.

The Body Has a Head

October 27

Sylvia Plath
(b. 1932 - d. February 11,1963)
American Poet

Perfection is terrible, it cannot have children.

"The Munich Mannequins"

October 28

Charles Francis Potter
(b. 1885 - d. October 4, 1962)
American Clergyman

The bird of war is not the eagle, but the stork.

The Preacher and I

October 29

Jean Giraudoux
(b. 1882 - d. January 31, 1944)
French Playwright

If two people who love each other let a single instant wedge itself between them, it grows — it becomes a month, a year, a century; it becomes too late.

The Madwoman of Chaillot

October 30

Henry S. Dennis
(b. 1938 -   )
American Dentist

Is liberty worth your son's life?

Personal Conversation

October 31

John Keats
(b. 1795 - d. February 23, 1821)
English Poet

The Setting Sun will always set me to rights, or if a Sparrow come before my Window, I take part in its existence and pick about the gravel.

Letter of November 22, 1817

It was November - the most lonely month
of the year.

Hillaire Belloc

November 1

Stephen Crane
(b. 1871 - d. June 5, 1900)
American Novelist and Poet

A man said to the universe,
"Sir, I exist!"
"However," replied the universe,
"The fact has not created in me
A sense of obligation."

"The Man"

November 2

Stephen de Grellet
(b. 1773 - d. November 16, 1855)
American Clergyman and Prison Reformer

I shall pass through this world but once. If therefore there be any kindness I can show, or any good thing I can do, let me do it now...for I shall not pass this way again.

Friendly Heritage

November 3

Andre Malraux
(b. 1901 - d. November 23, 1976)
French Writer

The great mystery is not that we have been flung at random between the profusion of matter and of the stars; but that within this prison we can draw from ourselves images powerful enough to deny our nothingness.

Anti-Memoirs

November 4

Will Rogers
(b. 1879 - d. August 15,1935)
American Humorist

Us ignorant laugh at spiritualists but when they die they go mighty peaceful and happy.   After all, all there is to living is to go away satisfied.

The Will Rogers Book

November 5

Will Durant
(b. 1885 -   )
American Historian

When liberty exceeds intelligence it begets chaos, which begets dictatorship.

This I Believe

November 6

James Jones
(b. 1921 - d. May 9, 1977)
American Novelist

There're so many guys, you know — young Americans and yes, young men everywhere — a whole generation of people younger than me who have grown up feeling inadequate as men because they haven't been able to fight in a war and find out whether they are brave or not. Because it is an effort to prove this bravery that we fight — in wars or in bars — whereas if a man were truly brave he wouldn't have to be always proving it to himself.

Writers at Work. series 3

November 7

Albert Camus
(b. 1913 - d. January 4, 1960)
French Writer

Do not select a life, but make the one you have stretch out...commit yourself completely. Then, show equal strength in accepting both yes and no.

Notebook I

Ivan Turgenev
November 9

November 8

George Earle Lytton
(b. 1831 - d. November 21, 1891)
English Writer

There is nothing so trivial in this world but what there will be some one to whom it is important.

The Parisians

November 9

Ivan Turgenev
(b. 1818 - d. September 3, 1883)
Russian Novelist

...if we wait for the moment when everything, absolutely everything is ready, we shall never begin.

The Virgin Soil

November 10

Oliver Goldsmith
(b. 1728 - d. April 4, 1774)
Irish Poet

The true use of speech is not so much to express our wants as to conceal them.

"The Bee"

November 11

Marquis of Halifax
(b. 1633 - d. April 5, 1695)
English Statesman

To understand the World, and to like it, are two things not easily to be reconciled.

Moral Thoughts and Reflections

November 12

August Rodin
(b. 1840 - d. November 17, 1917)
French Sculptor

Everywhere the great artist hears spirit answer to his spirit. Where, then, can you find a more religious man?

Art

November 13

Robert Louis Stevenson
(b. 1850 - d. December 3, 1894)
Scottish Writer

If your morals make you dreary, depend upon it they are wrong. I do not say "give them up," for they may be all you have; but conceal them like a vice, lest they should spoil the lives of better and simpler people.

"A Christmas Sermon"

November 14

Marya Mannes
(b. 1904 -   )
American Writer

Brave or not, it is imperative for this adult generation to make death a matter of life to their children. It is more than possible that their whole concept of dying has been warped either by the silence surrounding it, the attitudes of their family, or the chronic dosage of death by violence on television and movies.

Last Rights

November 15

Marianne Moore
(b. 1887 - d. February 5, 1972)
American Poet and Critic

    As contagion
  of sickness makes sickness,
contagion of trust can make trust.

"In Distrust of Merits"

November 16

Leon Daudet
(b. 1868 - d. July 1, 1942)
French Writer

The man of action is he in whom mental images have the strongest tendency to become real.

Alphonse Daudet

November 17

Hans Zinsser
(b. 1878 - d. September 4, 1940)

...it is a strange and terrifying thought that a human life — long and adventurous, full of joy and sorrow, effort and disappointment, pregnant with possibilities for good and evil, for suffering, for vice and virtue — should be begotten more or less accidentally, for no particular reason accept the enchantment of an early harvest moon.

As I Remember Him

November 18

Lord Moulton
(b. 1844 - d. March 9, 1921)
English Jurist and Scientist

Mere obedience to Law does not measure the greatness of a Nation....The true test is the extent to which the individuals composing the nation can be trusted to obey self-imposed law.

"Law and Manners"

November 19

Martin Luther
(b. 1483 - d. February 18, 1546)
German Theologian

Unthankfulness is theft.

Watchwords for the Warfare of Life

November 20

Alistair Cooke
(b. 1908 -   )
British/American Journalist

...we suffer just now from a tug of war between the theory and the practice of American life. We believe in patriotism and unselfish public service, but we imbue our children with the idea that material success is the real goal. Our children consequently live in a puzzled shadow between our ideals and our habits.

Speech of November 15, 1951

November 21

Voltaire
(b. 1694 - d. May 30, 1778)
French Philosopher

If God did not exist, we would have to invent him.

Letter of November 1, 1770

November 22

George Eliot
(b. 1819 - d. December 22, 1880)
American Writer

Our life is determined for us — and it makes the mind very free when we give up wishing, and only think of bearing what is laid upon us, and doing what is given us to do.

The Mill on the Floss

November 23

Harpo Marx
(b. 1888 - d. September 28, 1964)
American Actor and Harpist

The passing of an ordinary man is sad. The passing of a great man is tragic, and doubly tragic when the greatness passes before the man does.

Harpo Speaks

November 24

Benedict de Spinoza
(b. 1632 - d. February 21, 1677)
Dutch Philosopher

The virtue of a free man is seen to be as great in avoiding danger as in overcoming it.

Ethics

November 25

Joseph Wood Krutch
(b. 1893 - d. May 22, 1970)
American Writer

...the theory that children should be made to feel absolutely secure and perpetually surrounded by love used to strike me as dubious. It would give them, it seemed to me, a very false idea of what the world is like....But perhaps perfect security at the right time makes for boldness in the future, and perhaps to meet distress too early is to be made forever timid.

The Best of Two Worlds

November 26

Charles Schulz
(b. 1922 -   )
American Cartoonist

My life has no purpose...my life has no direction...no
aim...no meaning...and yet I'm happy...I can't figure
it out...What am I doing right?

It's a Long Way to Tipperary

November 27

James Agee
(b. 1909 - d. May 16, 1955)
American Writer

How awful, pitiful, beyond words it must be, to be so
terribly anxious for others, for others' good, and not
be able to do anything, even to say so. Not even to
help.

A Death in the Family

November 28

William Blake
(b. 1757 - d. August 12, 1827)
English Poet and Artist

He who binds to himself a joy
Does the winged life destroy;
But he who kisses the joy as it flies
Lives in eternity's sun rise.

"Eternity"

November 29

Wendell Philips
(b. 1811 - d. February 2, 1884)
American Writer

How "prudently" most men creep into nameless graves;
while now and then one or two forget themselves into
immortality.

"National Anti-Slavery Standard"

November 30

Mark Twain
(b. 1835 - d. April 21, 1910)
American Writer and Humorist

It is the goodness of God that in our country we have
those three unspeakably precious things: freedom of
speech, freedom of conscience, and the prudence never
to exercise either of them.

Following the Equator

November 31

Justin Thyme
(b. 1854 - d. February 29, 1978)
American Poet

Thirty days has September,
April, June and, Never mind.

"Here It Is"

This December I have been more aware than ever before of the meaning of a festival of light coming as it does when the days are so short, and we live in darkness for the greater part of the afternoon.

May Sarton

December 1

Woody Allen
(b. 1935 -   )
American Clarinetist

The universe is merely a fleeting idea in God's mind — a pretty uncomfortable thought, particularly if you've just made a down payment on a house.

Getting Even

December 2

Nikos Kazantzakis
(b. 1885 - d. October 26, 1957)
Greek Writer

Our daily cares lead us astray. A few people only, the flower of humanity, manage to live an eternity even in their transitory lives on this earth. Since all the others would therefore be lost, God had mercy on them and sent them religion — thus the crowd is able to live in eternity, too.

Zorba the Greek

December 3

Joseph Conrad
(b. 1857 - d. August 3, 1924)
English Novelist

...being myself animated by feelings of affection toward my fellow-men, I am saddened by the modern system of advertising. Whatever evidence it offers of enterprise, ingenuity, impudence, and resource in certain individuals, it proves to my mind the wide prevalence of that form of mental degradation which is called gullibility.

"An Anarchist"

Joseph Conrad

December 4

Ranier Maria Rilke
(b. 1875 - d. December 29,1926)
German Poet

...be patient toward all that is unsolved in your heart and try to love the *questions themselves....Live* the questions now. Perhaps you will then gradually, without noticing it, live along some distant day into the answer.

Letters to a Young Poet

December 5

Wassily Kandinsky
(b. 1866 - d. December 17,1944)
Russian Painter

Every work of art is the child of its time; often it is the mother of our emotions.

Concerning the Spiritual Art

December 6

Kahlil Gibran
(b. 1883 - d. April 10,1931)
Lebanese/American Poet

Keep me away from the wisdom which does not cry,
the philosophy which does not laugh and the greatness
which does not bow before children.

Mirrors of the Soul

December 7

Willa Cather
(b. 1873 - d. April 24,1947)
American Novelist

The generation now in the driver's seat hates to make
anything, wants to live and die in an automobile,
scudding past those acres where the old men used to
follow the long corn-rows up and down. They want
to buy everything ready-made: clothes, food, education,
music, pleasure. Will the third generation — the full-
blooded, joyous one just coming over the hill — will
it be fooled? Will it believe that to live easily is to
live happily?

"Nebraska"

December 8

Norman Douglas
(b. 1868 - d. February 9, 1952)
British Novelist and Scientist

...to find a friend one must close one eye: to keep him — two.

South Wind

December 9

John Milton
(b. 1608 - d. November 8, 1674)
English Poet

Give me the liberty to know, to utter, and to argue freely according to conscience above all liberties.... Let Truth and falsehood grapple; who ever knew Truth put to the worse in free and open encounter?

"Areopagitica"

Norman Douglas

December 10

Jonathan Swift
(b. 1667 - d. October 19, 1745)
English Satirist

We have just religion enough to make us hate, but not enough to make us love one another.

Miscellanies

December 11

Aleksandr I. Solzhenitsyn
(b. 1918 -)
Soviet Novelist and Historian

Own only what you can always carry with you: know languages, know countries, know people. Let your memory be your travel bag. Use your memory! It is those bitter seeds alone which might sprout and grow someday.

Gulag Archipelago

December 12

Gustav Flaubert
(b. 1821 - d. May 8, 1880)
French Novelist

A little science takes your religion from you; a great deal brings you back to it.

The Dictionary of Accepted Ideas

December 13

Lucy Freeman
(b. 1916 -   )
American Writer

Some people stand on the sidelines and observe life; others plunge into the sea of sensation, rarely to leave it....The one risks the danger of not living; the other, of living too intensely and, in that living, enduring torment on torment....The wise man will dip into the sea every now and then as he chooses, also spending time in the solitude of shore.

Fight Against Fears

December 14

Michael de Nostradamus
(b. 1503 - d. July 2, 1566)
French Prophet

Happy is the country that has no history.

Oracles of Nostradamus

December 15

Betty Smith
(b. 1896 - d. January 17, 1972)
American Novelist

The child must have a secret world in which live things that never were. It is necessary that she *believe*. She must start out by believing in things not of this world. Then when the world becomes too ugly for living in, the child can reach back and live in her imagination.

A Tree Grows in Brooklyn

December 16

Jane Austen
(b. 1775 - d. July 18, 1817)
English Novelist

Everything nourishes what is strong already.

Pride and Prejudice

December 17

Ford Maddox Ford
(b. 1873 - d. June 26, 1939)
English Writer

It's getting back to a beginning of everything that matters. It doesn't matter where or even when. Then you go forward with courage. That's what's the matter with today and here. We go forward into doubt because there's nothing but doubts into which to go forward. Faith is a thing you cannot borrow.

Ladies Whose Bright Eyes

December 18

Christopher Fry
(b. 1907 -   )
English Playwright

> ...laughter is surely
> The surest touch of genius in creation.
> Would *you* ever have thought of it, I ask you,
> If you had been making man...?

The Lady's Not for Burning

December 19

Edith Piaf
(b. 1915 - d. October 11, 1963)
French Singer

When you reach the top yourself you have to send the elevator back down so that others can also get to the top.

Quoted by Adlai Stevenson

December 20

George MacDonald
(b. 1824 - d. September 18, 1905)
Scottish Novelist

People must believe what they can, and those who believe more must not be hard on those who believe less.

The Princess and the Goblin

December 21

Benjamin Disraeli
(b. 1804 - d. April 19, 1881)
English Novelist and Historian

Man is only truly great when he acts from the passions; never irresistible but when he appeals to the imagination.

Coninsby

December 22

E.A. Robinson
(b. 1869 - d. April 5, 1935)
American Poet

       for every gift
Or sacrifice, there are...or there may be —
Two kinds of gratitude: the sudden kind
We feel for what we take, the larger kind
We feel for what we give.

"Captain Craig"

December 23

Charles Augustin Sainte-Beuve
(b. 1804 - d. October 13, 1869)
French Critic

Tell me who admires and loves you, and I will tell you who you are.

"On Sainte-Beuve's Method"

December 24

Giles French
(b. 1894 - d. June 30, 1976)
American Journalist

Give a man a few crumbs and he will appreciate them.
Give him a cake and he will complain about the
flavoring.

The Things We Note

December 25

Jesus of Nazareth
(b. 4 B.C. - d. April 6, 30 A.D.)
Founder of Christianity

Blessed are the meek, for they shall inherit the earth.

Sermon on the Mount

December 26

Henry Miller
(b. 1891 -   )
American Writer

In the range of invention, if not in the *powers* of invention, the man of today is nearer to being a god than at any time in his history. (So we like to believe!) Yet never was he less godlike. He accepts and utilizes the miraculous gifts of science unquestioningly; he is without wonder, without awe, reverence, zest, vitality or joy. He draws no conclusions from the past, has no peace or satisfaction in the present, and is utterly unconcerned about the future. He is marking time. That is about the most we can say for him.

The Books in My Life

December 27

Johannes Kepler
(b. 1571 - d. November 15, 1630)
German Astronomer

The roads that lead man to knowledge are as wondrous as that knowledge itself.

Quoted by Arthur Koestler

December 28

Woodrow Wilson
(b. 1856 - d. February 3, 1924)
United States President

There is such a thing as a nation being so right that it does not need to convince others by force that it is right.

Speech of May 10, 1915

December 29

E.H. Chapin
(b. 1814 - d. December 26, 1880)
American Clergyman

A true man never frets about his place in the world, but just slides into it by the gravitation of his nature, and swings there as easily as a star.

Living Words

December 30

Rudyard Kipling
(b. 1865 - d. January 18, 1936)
English Writer

When your Daemon is in charge, do not try to think consciously. Drift, wait, and obey.

Something of Myself

December 31

Holbrook Jackson
(b. 1874 - d. June 16, 1948)
English Essayist

Posterity is coming into its own — you can almost hear the future chuckling with satisfaction.

"Standing by Posterity"

ACKNOWLEDGMENTS

I am most indebted to the 367 people represented on the preceding pages and their mothers who so conveniently gave birth to them on evenly distributed days throughout the year. But my indebtedness does not end here.

I owe thanks to every person I know and most of the strangers I've encountered over a three year period. These quotations weren't just chosen at random. They were voted on by hundreds of people who went through stacks of little note cards marking the ones they felt were the most discussible.

I haven't entered anyone's home in the last three years without going through their bookshelves (you wouldn't believe the dust) in an attempt to find underlined passages.

I've attended every church library in Portland, and every college and county library in the Pacific Northwest, asking unending and tedious questions of the librarians ("surely you *must* know when Walter Benjamin died!")

This is my chance to say "thank you," or perhaps, "I'm sorry," to all the people waiting at bus stops, sitting in restaurants, hotel lobbies, walking peacefully down city streets, and making love in the parks, whom I've asked to read quotes for me and vote on the ones they've liked best.

And to those of you who didn't run when you saw me coming a second time I say, "What endurance!"

To the grocery clerks who have had to put up with "Did you celebrate George Horace Lorimer's birthday today?" what customer service.

To the bank tellers who couldn't quite close their windows before I got to them, and faced a "please cash this check and choose between these ten quotes by W.N.P. Barbellion," (who on earth is he anyhow?), what courage!

To my fellow committee and board members who have had to put up with "I'll second the motion if you'll read these quotes," now wasn't it worth it?

For those of you who have invited me to parties over these past few years and have had forced entertainment in the form of group reading, what hostmanship.

To the owners of the second-hand bookstores who've probably

suspected me of shop-lifting until they've figured out it wouldn't take eight hours to lift a book, I'm sorry I'm such a slow reader.

To my mother and father, thank you for giving me a birthday of my own so I wouldn't feel left out. I love sharing it with Willa Cather! And I thank my aunties, Helen and Mary, and again my parents, for sharing every college note and diary going back to 1918 (it runs in the family, you see) — aren't you glad you don't throw anything away?

To my husband, Doug, thank you for so generously sharing our bed with Thoreau, Keats, Nietszche, and the hundreds of other volumes that have lined the sheets, and for tolerating the flashlight underneath the covers; the Chopin and company in the wee hours, and never ever seeing me in the mornings, at least awake.

To my children, Austin, Trevor and Marya, who turning 6, 7, and 8, have learned that when mommy's not busy writing books she cleans house and mends clothes and cooks fancy food. But that's usually at 3 a.m. and certainly not very often. Oh, but moms have fun and are never bored, now, are they dears?

In all seriousness, I am very grateful to all my friends and family for their time, loving support and especially their enthusiasm for this book. I am indebted most of all to my co-publisher, Dick Willis, for all his hard work, time, and patience. (I am equally indebted to his family for the sacrifices they've had to make.)

The artwork by Joelle Smith has been a beautiful contribution to *Quotidian*, and the cover design by my uncle, Hal Johnson, a special touch. Ginny Bass, Cathy Peyton, Jackie Hoag, Doug and Paula Davina, Phil Bass, Liz Austin, Mike Finley, Julie Dennis, Robin Rifer, Carol Turner, Lyle Ashcraft, Phyllis Elliott and Spence Meighan contributed a great deal of time towards the selection of the quotes. My sister, Holly Johnson, Vern Rifer, Mark Bershadsky, Jolly Butler, Liz Gill, Pam Horan, my mother-in-law, Barbara Cable, and Sherry and Dave Redford were indispensible in the final production stages.

Christopher Morley, wherever you are, I adore you!

INDEX